# ACTIVITY BOOK

*Peter Viney and Karen Viney*

Oxford University Press

Oxford University Press
Walton Street, Oxford OX2 6DP

Oxford University Press
200 Madison Avenue, New York, NY 10016 USA

Oxford  New York
Athens  Auckland  Bangkok  Bombay
Calcutta  Cape Town  Dar es Salaam  Delhi
Florence  Hong Kong  Istanbul  Karachi
Kuala Lumpur  Madras  Madrid  Melbourne
Mexico City  Nairobi  Paris  Singapore
Taipei  Tokyo  Toronto

and associated companies in
Berlin  Ibadan

OXFORD and OXFORD ENGLISH are trade marks of
Oxford University Press

First published 1995
Second impression 1996

ISBN 0 19 458850 5  (Activity Book)

ISBN 0 19 458851 3  (VHS PAL Video Cassette 1)
ISBN 0 19 458852 1  (VHS PAL Video Cassette 2)
ISBN 0 19 458853 X  (VHS SECAM Video Cassette 1)
ISBN 0 19 458854 8  (VHS SECAM Video Cassette 2)
ISBN 0 19 458855 6  (VHS NTSC Video Cassette 1)
ISBN 0 19 458856 4  (VHS NTSC Video Cassette 2)

ISBN 0 19 458857 2  (BETAMAX PAL Video Cassette 1)
ISBN 0 19 458858 0  (BETAMAX PAL Video Cassette 2)
ISBN 0 19 458859 9  (BETAMAX SECAM Video Cassette 1)
ISBN 0 19 458860 2  (BETAMAX SECAM Video Cassette 2)
ISBN 0 19 458861 0  (BETAMAX NTSC Video Cassette 1)
ISBN 0 19 458862 9  (BETAMAX NTSC Video Cassette 2)

© Oxford University Press, 1995

Printed in Hong Kong

## ACKNOWLEDGEMENTS

*Illustrations by:*
Antonia Enthoven
Ian Moores
Barry Wheat, Technical Graphics
Rob Hancock

*Video stills photography by*
Rob Judges

*Additional photography by*
Peter Viney

*Studio photography by*
Mark Mason

*The publishers would like to thank the following for their permission to
reproduce photographs:*

The Anthony Blake Photo Library
Caltrans
NYT Pictures
Retna Pictures Ltd
Rex Features Ltd/ Eugene Adebari, Lynn McAfee, Neil Preston
Topham

A video such as this involves the creative efforts of many people,
and we wish to thank the actors and crew for all their work. We
would like to add a personal acknowledgment to Robert Maidment
who worked closely with us from the earliest script drafts and not
only produced but directed *Only in America*, as well as to our
editors Ken Mencz (script) and Tim Blakey (Activity Book),
and to Phil Hall for designing the Activity Book.

*Peter Viney & Karen Viney*

# Contents

### Duane and Donna in New York    10

□□:□□

numbers; ordinal numbers; the alphabet; *a / an*; the verb *to be*, present tense; questions – *who? where? how much?*; pronouns and possessive adjectives; greetings
**Vocabulary:** telephoning, hotels, signs

### First Day    18

□□:□□

*There is some... / There are some...* ; *any? / not... any*; countable and uncountable nouns; possessive adjectives; sequence words; adjectives; prepositions of place; introductions; forms of address
**Vocabulary:** food; items on a table for meals; restaurants

### Strange Encounter    26

□□:□□

*have* present tense (*Do you have...?*; *I don't have...*); imperatives; object pronouns; describing people; present continuous tense for description; asking about prices
**Vocabulary:** describing people; photography; U.S. money

### Big Deal!    34

□□:□□

*would like*; requests with *Could...? / May...? / Can...?*; giving directions; *Which?*; *one / ones* (*the red one / these ones*); review of *have* and sequence words.
**Vocabulary:** house and pool; salads and salad dressings; nationalities

### Office Blues    42

□□:□□

*can / can't* for permission and ability; present continuous tense; *going to* for future reference; present and future time words; *When?*; contractions in speech
**Vocabulary:** office equipment; parties

### The Websters    50

□□:□□

present simple tense; everyday habits; frequency adverbs; questions about frequency, *How often?*; *Do you ever...?*; dates
**Vocabulary:** a family house; items in the kitchen; items in the bedroom

### Good Morning, Greenstown    58

□□:□□

*was / were*; past simple tense (*Did you do...?*; *I didn't go...*); regular and irregular verbs in the past; possessive pronouns
**Vocabulary:** audio equipment; music; past tenses; abbreviations

### The Artist    66

□□:□□

suggestions; arrangements; *let*; *want to do*; future simple tense (*I'll ...* , etc.); regular and irregular verbs in the past; *... , isn't it?*
**Vocabulary:** shapes and colors; location; prices and value; describing people

# To the teacher

## *Only in America*

*Only in America* is a course in American English for beginners, consisting of:

**Only in America Activity Book,**

**Only in America videos.** (Eight short video stories, on two cassettes, available in VHS or Betamax formats to NTSC, PAL, and SECAM standards.)

*Only in America* can be used in a variety of teaching situations:
- **to accompany any beginner's course**

There is no continuing story, and each of the eight videos can be used separately from the rest of the materials, and in any sequence. Each video story has been designed to focus on major structural areas normally studied at this level. See "Contents" on page 3 for integrating the materials with your course.
- **to accompany** *Main Street 1* **and** *Main Street 2*

The syllabus is based on the *Main Street* series, also published by Oxford University Press. Teachers using *Main Street* might find the integration chart on page 7 useful.
- **as a short course**

*Only in America* also contains vocabulary, exercises and reference material that can be studied without access to video equipment. It can be used for anywhere between 8 and 40 hours, making it suitable as a short video led course in its own right.
- **at higher levels**

Video can always be used at a higher level than that of the structures used in presentation material, as much of the work relates to the visuals and situations. There are specific notes on adapting the materials for intermediate students on pages 6 to 9.

## Using the *Only in America* Activity Book

For each of the eight video stories the Activity Book contains:
- **Watching the video.** Four pages of activities for classroom exploitation. If you only follow the activities suggested, you will have a thorough exploitation of the materials. If you have more time with video, you can add some of the activities suggested below under "Teaching with video: some techniques." There are specific notes for teachers on each of the videos on pages 6 to 9. Most units are viewed throughout, then exploited in four separate sections, followed by viewing of the complete story again. There are three categories of activity: BEFORE YOU WATCH, WHILE YOU WATCH, and AFTER YOU WATCH. Each story ends with a free IMAGINE ... activity based on the story.
- **Vocabulary.** This section can be used at any time during work on a particular video for reference, or after watching the video as further exercises with a vocabulary bias.
- **Tell the story.** A page of pictures taken from the video. These can be used in a number of ways, from paired retelling of parts of the video during initial presentation to review and consolidation after work with each video.
- **Exercises.** These are related to the story of the video, but can be done after the initial exploitation, without access to video equipment. They also contain exercises which highlight the structural content of the videos.
- **Reference.** A complete language summary of each video for reference.
- **Transcripts** of the dialogue can be found on pages 74 to 80. These should not be used in class, but in our experience students wish to have a transcript to which they can refer after the lesson.

## Instructional language

We have not confined instructional language (printed in bold italics) to the level of the materials. The possibilities with video are such that we think it worth the teacher getting more complex instructions across to the students. Ideally this would be done by demonstration and example. As a last resort, they may be translated.

## Teaching with video, some techniques:

### LOCATING THE PLACE ON THE TAPE

Many modern VCRs have a minutes and seconds counter. Sections have a time reference in minutes and seconds in the Activity Book. Each episode begins at 00.00. If your VCR has an older counter, note the counter numbers for the beginning of each section on the contents page, and at the head of sections. Counter numbers will only work if you rewind the tape to the beginning and zero the counter each time you use the tape. If you have a minutes and seconds counter, you will only need to zero the counter at the beginning of each episode. Press RESET as the first picture appears after the *Only in America* logo. If you have MEMORY, the tape will return to this point whenever you REWIND. You can reset the counter after each section.

There are two types of REWIND (<<) and FAST FORWARD (>>) on most VCRs. The ones labelled REWIND/FAST FORWARD blank out the picture. Ones labelled CUE/ REVIEW or PICTURE SEARCH enable the picture to be seen at speed during rewinding and fast forwarding. Apart from finding the place, these facilities can be used to remind students of parts of the story, or to review what has already been covered if there is a gap between lessons.

### FREEZE FRAMING (STILL PICTURE) ACTIVITIES

Freeze framing means stopping the picture, using the FREEZE FRAME, STILL or PAUSE (II or > I <) control. This will not harm the videotape, all VCRs are designed to release the freeze frame automatically before any damage can be done. Freeze frame is the most important feature on VCRs in the classroom, and should be the main criterion in selecting a particular VCR. A remote control is also important.

Modern VCRs have near perfect freeze frame, look out for SUPER STILL, or PERFECT STILL. Older VCRs may judder and have white lines. The irritation of these can be relieved by pressing the freeze frame control once or twice, moving the white line to a less important part of the picture. A few light taps on the machine will often shift the white line on older VCRs.

FRAME ADVANCE or STILL ADVANCE is a useful control found on many VCRs, moving the still picture forward one frame at a time. It can be used to explore the nuances of an event or of a facial reaction. JOG/SHUTTLE can be found on some VCRs and is a rotary control which enables you to move the picture forwards or backward as if by hand at various speeds.

- **Comprehension questions**

You can freeze frame at any time to check comprehension.
- **Using the background**

Video contains 25-30 pictures per second, and there is a wealth of detail in the background of the pictures which can be exploited through freeze framing. Teachers will often find something new even when they have done a particular lesson many times over. The background also gives access to material about American life and culture. For example students may be interested in the house in *The Websters*, or the diner in *First Day*. One of the major differences between programs designed for TV broadcast, and videos like *Only in America* designed for classroom use, lies in the presumption of the teacher's ability to use freeze frame to explore and exploit background detail. The camera does not need to linger on things in the background, as they can always be singled out later with freeze frame.

● **Vocabulary**

You can freeze frame to check vocabulary items in the picture.

● **Prediction (What next?)**

Prediction occurs when freeze framing is used during the initial viewing of a section. You can freeze frame and ask about either EVENTS (*What's going to happen?*) or DIALOGUE (*What are they saying? / What are they going to say next?*).

● **Retelling**

When students have already seen a section, they will be using memory to retell either what is being said, or to describe what is happening, or what has just happened.

● **Body language**

Video gives us an additional exploitable dimension of information about body language, facial expressions, gesture, stance, reaction and response. See Laura in *Office Blues*, or Tony Vidal in *Big Deal!*

● **Thoughts and emotions**

Freeze frame and ask about feelings and emotions. This can also involve judgement on whether characters are telling the truth or not. You can ask students to imagine additional information about the characters, based on what they have deduced from the video.

## SEPARATING SOUND AND VISION

You can separate sound and vision by turning down sound on the monitor, by using the mute control, or by obscuring the screen with a coat, piece of cloth or card.

● **Vision only activities**

A number of vision only activities are suggested in the Activity Book. Several sequences are purely visual. See for example *First Day* section 3, and *The Artist* section 3. There is no need to remove sound. Music is usually present during these sequences.

● **Silent viewing**

Silent viewing means removing an existing soundtrack before making use of the visuals on their own. Silent viewing will be a PREDICTION technique when students are viewing for the first time, and a RETELLING technique when they have already seen and heard the section being used for silent viewing.

● **Silent viewing for prediction**

Students can talk about EVENTS (*What's happening on the screen?*) or DIALOGUE (*What are they saying?*). They will be able to predict dialogue, i.e. guess what people are saying, throughout the course. For example, we often see one side of a telephone dialogue, and students have to supply the other side.

● **Silent viewing for retelling**

Retelling can be divided into RETELLING DIALOGUE and RETELLING EVENTS. Retelling dialogue is most effective where there are useful formulas, fixed expressions and points of intonation or pronunciation. Retelling events tends to focus on narrative tenses, and on sequences.

● **Random sound down (Cloze listening)**

This may be done at any time, but is particularly suitable when viewing the whole episode again. Turn the sound down at random intervals asking students to fill in the missing dialogue.

● **Sound only activities**

You can play a section of one of the videos with the picture obscured so that they hear the dialogue but are unable to see the action. Students can be asked either to predict what is happening visually, or to use the soundtrack as a memory spur to recall what happened visually. See "Random sound down" above. A parallel activity can also be done by obscuring the picture with card at random intervals.

## PRONUNCIATION

Because the actors' gestures and expressions can be seen, you can do work on pronunciation, stress, rhythm and intonation by imitating the voices on the video. Teachers may wish to do repetition work on selected lines from the dialogues.

## PAIRED VIEWING ACTIVITIES

Paired activities take more effort in setting up, but the results justify the effort.

● **Description**

One student in each pair closes their eyes or turns their back to the screen. The other student faces the screen, and the video is played silently. The student who can see the screen describes the action to their partner. Both students will wish to hear the soundtrack later. The "passive" student in each pair will be motivated to see what they have missed as well. It is worth making sure that the partners change roles, or that the activity is done twice, with different sections so that each partner gets a chance to perform the "active" role.

● **Narration**

This requires organisation, as it involves sending half the class out of the room while the remaining half watch a section of a video. When they return, they are told about the video in pairs by those who saw it. (See the note above about changing roles.) This could be done by team teaching, working with two parallel classes at the same time.

● **Split class: Description/Narration**

Half the class is sent out. The remainder watch a section silently. Then the two halves change places. The ones that were outside now listen to the same section with the picture covered (see "Sound only activities," above). The students are then paired off. One student in each pair has <u>seen</u> the video, but <u>hasn't heard</u> the dialogue. The other student has only <u>heard</u> the dialogue. They work together to piece the story together. The "Tell the story" section in the Activity Book can be used as a basis for this.

## ROLE-PLAYS

Students can be asked to role-play sequences they have seen in the videos.

We have found it more productive to get them to role play things which are <u>not seen</u> in the video, but which they can guess from having seen the video, e.g., the conversation when Scott collects the pictures in *Strange Encounter*.

# The video classroom

We have found that most video equipment in schools is linked to monitors simply using the antenna connectors. This impairs quality needlessly when most equipment has either separate video and audio connectors (RCA connectors), a multi-pin Euroconnector (SCART), or S-VHS connectors. The use of these connections should bring about an improvement in picture and audio quality. Refer to the manuals for your equipment, a copy of which should be kept with the equipment in case of problems. Incidentally, the most common difficulty we have found is that many TVs revert to Channel 1 when they are turned off, often making it necessary to reselect the video channel. This does not matter when the VCR is connected by means of a special connector. Another common irritation is noise and white lines on the blank screen when the VCR is stopped, or even worse a TV channel. This can be eliminated entirely by selecting LINE or AV on the VCR rather than TUNER. There will then be no need to switch off the TV between activities. Note that video equipment should be positioned so as not to expose it to boardwriter or chalk dust.

# Teacher's notes

If you have only one lesson for exploiting each story, you should simply follow the *Watching the video* section in the Activity Book. If you have more time, you can add some of the activities suggested in the detailed notes below.

**Notes** give cultural information.

**Section 1, Section 2,** etc. give ideas for activities in addition to those in the Activity Book. The activities assume that students have little or no knowledge beyond the points listed in the reference section for each story. For scope and sequence, please see the Contents on page 3.

Video can be used with great success at levels higher than the level of the actual dialogue material. We suggest some ideas under the heading "Higher levels."

## □□ : □□ Duane and Donna in New York

**New York Quiz.** The purpose of this quiz is to tune the students in to New York and the U.S.A. and check on the use of the verb "to be."

New York Quiz answers:
1) 8 million 2) Washington 3) east coast 4) yellow 5) Big Apple 6) I love NY 7) NYC 8) skyscrapers

**Notes:**
1 Minnesota is a state in the Midwest, about 1200 miles (1900 km) from New York City.
2 Refer to page 16 for the map of New York City and pictures of buildings – we see the Chrysler Building, the Trump Tower, Grand Central Terminal and Central Park in the video. The purpose of the story is not a travelogue of NYC, and we suggest avoiding too much "local" information.
3 The limo(usine) outside the hotel is a "stretch limo."

**Section 1**
Use paired description for retelling on second viewing.
**Section 2**
Freeze frame for vocabulary.
**Section 3**
Freeze frame during telephone dialogues. Students predict other side freely.
**Section 4**
Paired description for retelling on second viewing.

**Higher levels**
1 Discussion point – young people traveling together; student vacation times; student dress; staying casually with friends.
2 Ask students to describe people and clothing throughout. Use the present continuous for actions
3 Narrative tenses (e.g.: present simple, past simple) can be used in "Tell the story."
4 Focus on Donna and Duane reacting while the other is speaking. Ask about their thoughts and feelings.
5 Paired description on initial viewing can be done with sections 1 and 4.

**Tell the story**
Beginners will not be able to use narrative tenses, but they can suggest a line of dialogue, or a simple statement (*They're near the subway exit. / This is Duane's digital diary.*)

## □□ : □□ First Day

**Notes:**
1 Americans eat out often, and food in diners and fast food outlets is inexpensive.
2 There was some disagreement about the exact constituents of a club sandwich (e.g.: some preferred ham rather than bacon). We used a consensus opinion, which was also the exact recipe at the diner where we taped the story.
3 American students often pay their way through college by taking part-time work.
4 Point out food hygiene regulations – plastic gloves (rings can break the gloves).

**Section 1**
Freeze frame to recall dialogue on second viewing.
**Section 2**
Expand, explain vocabulary using freeze frame.
**Section 3**
This is a vision only activity – if you freeze frame to slow the action, it's best to have sound off. Do "While you watch" in pairs.
**Section 4**
Freeze frame on expressions – guess what they are saying to themselves (cf. "Imagine" section).

**Higher levels**
1 Watch in sections without viewing the whole story first.
2 Ask students to describe people and clothing throughout. Begin: Ashley: *How is it?*
3 Have students deduce facts about Ashley from her car / clothing before she begins speaking.
4 Narrative tenses (e.g.: present simple, past simple) can be used in "Tell the story." Focus on sequence words introduced in the story during this.
5 Focus on reactions and facial expressions, especially in the Ashley / Tammy dialogue, and on Mr. Winthrop's facial contortions at the end.
6 Ask: *Why is it important that Winthrop is a lawyer?* (he can sue) *What are they afraid of?*
7 Discuss uniforms, name tags, etc.

**Tell the story**
Beginners will not be able to use narrative tenses. They can however suggest a line of dialogue, or a simple statement.

| Video story | Relationship to *Main Street* |
|---|---|
| Duane and Donna in New York | Main Street 1, units 1 to 5 |
| First Day | Main Street 1, units 6 to 10 |
| Strange Encounter | Main Street 1, units 11 to 15 |
| Big Deal! | Main Street 1, units 16 to 20 |
| Office Blues | Main Street 2, units 1 to 5 |
| The Websters | Main Street 2, units 6 to 10 |
| Good morning, Greenstown | Main Street 2, units 11 to 15 |
| The Artist | Main Street 2, units 16 to 20 |

## □□:□□ Strange Encounter

There are five sections instead of four, and we suggest exploiting section by section **without** previewing. You can view the whole story first with weaker groups.

**Notes:**
1 The story was taped on the south coast of Long Island, NY. Rockport is fictitious, but was based on summer resort towns (the Hamptons).
2 Photo store + vocabulary U.S. money. Because U.S. bills are all one color, store clerks often say "Out of twenty" to avoid later disputes.
3 "That's a nice name" – some Americans often compliment on clothes, name, etc. on initial meeting.
4 "guys" – once used for males only, but now unisex.

**Section 1**
Initially view silently for prediction plus vocabulary (*dunes, beach, sand, ocean,*).
**Section 2**
Freeze frame to explore background vocabulary.
**Section 3**
Freeze frame or silent viewing to elicit next line of dialogue (either as retelling or prediction) in photo store.
**Section 4**
Freeze frame to describe Officer, Scott, Britanny – then check with vocabulary page.
**Section 5**
Paired description on second viewing.

**Higher levels**
1 Paired description can be done with sections 1, 2 and 4 on initial viewing.
2 Sci-fi (science fiction) could be discussed at higher levels plus attitudes to aliens (horror / fear in the 1950s through benign in the 1980s, from "ET" onwards).
3 Investigate why Vega sounds alien (pauses, intonation, etc.). How could she sound more natural?
4 With much higher groups, discuss film techniques – cuts, angles, etc.
5 Refer to vocabulary during photo store dialogue and discuss advantages of different colors and sizes for bills (cf. Canada).
6 Discuss Britanny and Scott's emotions throughout.

**Tell the story**
Beginners will not be able to use narrative tenses. They can however suggest a line of dialogue, or a simple statement.

## □□:□□ Big Deal!

**Notes:**
1 Genre – a pastiche on the gangster movie, but with no violence, no bad language… and no crime!
2 This house is in a <u>very</u> wealthy neighborhood, but home pools are quite common in the hotter states.
3 See page 38 for the salads mentioned.
4 "Go ahead – Make his day!". This derives from a Clint Eastwood movie. His opponent goes for his gun – Eastwood says "Go ahead – Make my day!" (i.e. you'll give me an excuse to shoot you, and that'll make my day (a good day). It has been adopted for "Beware of the dog" signs.

**Section 1**
Paired description up to start of dialogue.
**Section 2**
Play silently initially – see how much of the story they pick up from body language / gesture.
**Section 3**
Silent viewing for retelling or freeze frame to elicit next line of dialogue on second viewing during meal order. Freeze frame during telephone call to elicit Olsen's words freely.
**Section 4**
Silent viewing or paired description for retelling.

**Higher levels**
1 Play in sections without viewing the whole story.
2 Paired description for sections 1 and 4, plus predict story after silent viewing of each section.
3 Discuss whether a crime is involved (*Are the computers stolen?*), or whether Vidal simply deals in cheap products.
4 Compare lifestyles.
5 Freeze frame and explore Vidal's body language.
6 Examine eye contact, etc. between Stephanie and Kevin in 1 and 4.
7 Go on to use end credits to review stories 1 to 4 (*What's happening in the credit shot?*).

**Tell the story**
Beginners will not be able to use narrative tenses. They can however suggest a line of dialogue, or a simple statement. At higher levels, the story can be retold using simple present narrative, present continuous description or past narrative.

# □□:□□ Office Blues

**Notes:**

1 The 21st birthday is a major milestone in the U.S. Twenty-one is the legal age for drinking alcohol in bars.

2 With business-orientated groups, compare office politics, roles, dress, and hierarchies as well as celebrations and parties.

3 Compare use of first names with the practice in the students' country – while noting that Ms. Revere's position is shown by the form of address. However, first names are used even for senior managers in many companies. Friendly informality is normal (though everyone still knows who is boss).

4 See page 49 "Reference" for notes on contractions.

**Pre-section 1**

Use opening credits to cover what was in stories 1 to 4 – they can guess which pieces come from *Office Blues*.

**Section 1**

Freeze frame for vocabulary (e.g.: *lobby, elevator, floor indicator, hall, entryphone,* etc. plus objects on Laura's desk (see "Before you watch," before watching the whole story).

**Section 2**

Silent viewing to retell dialogue on second viewing.

**Section 3**

Silent viewing initially to predict dialogue or play sound only initially. Either method will focus attention on Laura's body language. Then freeze frame to explore body language / eye contact. Have students act out scene (a) standing still with hands by their sides (b) using body language.

**Section 4**

Freeze frame to elicit other side of telephone call. Freeze frame for vocabulary.

**Higher levels**

1 Play in sections without viewing the whole story.

2 See notes – discuss heirarchy, dress, roles in Bruno's office. Guess what their jobs are and what the office does! Compare with offices in their country.

3 Contrast communication styles – Samuel's calmness and Ms. Revere's assertive manner.

**Tell the story**

Beginners will not be able to use narrative tenses, but now have access to the present continuous and "going to" future. This should be utilised here.

# □□:□□ The Websters

**Notes:**

1 The Websters' house is in a small town in New Jersey, about an hour from New York City. It's a typical middle-income neighborhood of older houses, and the house size is about average.

2 Paper boys and girls deliver newspapers in suburban neighborhoods.

3 High school students often have cars (distances in the U.S. are often comparatively large). With adults, car pools are more and more common.

4 As the video brings out, the famous hot cooked American breakfast is seen more on restaurant menus than in family homes – especially on weekdays. Note that each of the family is dealing with their own breakfast.

**Section 1**

Freeze frame to expand on vocabulary.

**Section 2**

Use sound only to provoke initial interest before exploiting the section.

**Section 3**

Freeze frame to elicit next line of dialogue (either as prediction or as retelling).

**Section 4**

Explore the meetings and greetings in more detail using freeze frame. Use silent viewing for retelling.

**Higher levels**

1 Play in sections without viewing the whole story.

2 Compare families at breakfast in different countries, and the way in which people interact in the video.

3 Use paired description for sections 1 and 4.

4 Expand frequency adverbs, adding *generally, normally, rarely, nearly always, almost never* while discussing everyday habits.

**Tell the story**

Beginners will not be able to use past tenses, but now have access to present simple for narration, as well as present continuous and "going to" future. At higher levels, straightforward past narration can be used, although this story emphasises the present simple for daily routines.

## ☐☐ : ☐☐ Good Morning, Greenstown

The Activity Book exploits this in four sections **without** viewing the whole story. With weaker groups you may wish to view the whole story initially.

It is possible to present the whole story first with sound only (though it becomes very long for audio presentation). If you do, play only the parts of the program that are transmitted, missing out the talk inside the studio. You will need to note counter / minute and second numbers to do this.

### Notes:
1  You can find notes on U.S. radio on page 62. Radio and TV stations have three or four letter IDs. IDs in the west begin with K (KHJ, Los Angeles), those in the east begin with W (WMCA, New York), those in Canada begin with C (CKST, Vancouver).
2  Greg Tyler's intoductory phrases (*your morning DJ, fighting the freeway,* etc.) are all taken from genuine radio shows.

### Section 1
Introduce sound only, up to: *Here's Tanisha ….* Ask students to describe Greg Tyler. Rewind and play normally.
### Section 2
Play sound only initially – so students don't see the problem over questions or freeze frame, have students predict (or retell) the quiz answers.
### Section 3
Play sound only initially – so students don't see the problem over questions.
### Section 4
Silent viewing for retelling dialogue.

### Higher levels
1  Run through the story again, focusing on Marcie's expressions and gestures. Freeze frame and discuss them.
2  At a much higher level, you could elicit reported speech and past perfect during "Tell the story."

### Tell the story
The simple past is now available for narration.

## ☐☐ : ☐☐ The Artist

Silent viewing for paired description works well with this story. You could do this with sections, or for the whole story.

### Notes:
1  Stroheim is fictional.
2  New York is probably the world's greatest center for modern art museums, and for galleries.
3  An *art museum* has several *galleries* for displaying art within it. A *gallery* is a commercial store displaying and selling works of art. In other English speaking countries, e.g.: Canada, an *art museum* would be called an *art gallery*.
4  The artist was at college in Kansas City, 1,230 miles (1,950 km) from New York on the Missouri River.
5  When retelling the story, point out that the size of pictures is given in art museum catalogs (the artist is looking at a catalog in section 2). The artist chose the Stroheim for its size.

### Section 1
Freeze frame to focus on reactions, body language, expressions. Ask about feelings – particularly as the artist is constantly anticipating the owner's reactions. *What does she hope she'll say?* v *What'll she say?* You might want to incorporate the dictionary exercise on page 70. Describe their clothes (note *scarf, pearls* – around the owner's neck).
### Section 2
Note the change in music at the start of section 2 – contrast with the section 1 music.
### Section 3
Silent viewing and / or paired description. Supply vocabulary – *stick, double-sided tape.* Describe the visitors who look at the picture.
### Section 4
Freeze frame to predict / retell next line of dialogue.

### Higher levels
1  Play in sections without viewing the whole story.
2  At a much higher level, you could elicit reported speech and past perfect during "Tell the story."
3  Contrast the accents of the gallery owner and the artist.

### Tell the story
The simple past is now available for narration.

*Video*

**ONE 1 ONE**

# Duane and Donna in New York

## BEFORE YOU WATCH

**Check ☑ the correct answers:**

1  The population of New York City is
   ☐ eight million
   ☐ eighteen million
   ☐ eighty million

**NEW YORK QUIZ**

2  The capital of the United States is
   ☐ Los Angeles
   ☐ Washington
   ☐ New York City

3  New York is
   ☐ on the west coast
   ☐ in the south
   ☐ on the east coast

4  New York taxi cabs are
   ☐ black
   ☐ yellow
   ☐ white

5  Another name for New York is
   ☐ The Big Cheese
   ☐ The Big City
   ☐ The Big Apple

6  I ♥ NY means
   ☐ New York is number one
   ☐ I love New York
   ☐ My heart is in New York

7  The business center of the U.S.A. is
   ☐ Washington
   ☐ Chicago
   ☐ New York City

8  New York is famous for
   ☐ skyscrapers
   ☐ good highways
   ☐ theme parks

**Watch Duane and Donna in New York.**

## AFTER YOU WATCH

**True or false? Check ✓ the boxes.**

|  |  | true | false |
|---|---|---|---|
| 1 | Duane and Donna are from Minnesota. | ☐ | ☐ |
| 2 | This is their last day in New York. | ☐ | ☐ |
| 3 | Duane and Donna are rich. | ☐ | ☐ |
| 4 | The hotel is expensive. | ☐ | ☐ |
| 5 | Duane and Donna are young. | ☐ | ☐ |
| 6 | The Trump Tower isn't in New York. | ☐ | ☐ |
| 7 | Duane and Donna don't know Max. | ☐ | ☐ |
| 8 | Max is a friend of Michael's. | ☐ | ☐ |

### SECTION 1  0 0 : 0 0

*(from the beginning to **Duane:** Wow! …)*

## BEFORE YOU WATCH

**Look at these words. Are they the same (or nearly the same) in your language? Write Y for yes, N for no.**

☐ restaurant    ☐ subway exit
☐ taxi    ☐ skyscraper
☐ hotel    ☐ jeans
☐ backpack    ☐ movie theater
☐ guide book    ☐ limo
☐ camera    ☐ escalator

## WHILE YOU WATCH

**<u>Underline</u> the things you see in the video.**

 **Watch section 1.**

## AFTER YOU WATCH

**1  Fill in the blanks.**

**Duane:** _____ here.
This _____ New York!

**Donna:** _____ Donna, **Duane:** _____ Duane,
and _____ Duane.   and _____ Donna.

**2  Answer these questions.**
Where are they?
What's his name?
What's her name?
Are they from New York?
Where are they from?

### SECTION 2  0 1 : 4 4

*(to **Duane:** …Where's a phone booth?)*

## WHILE YOU WATCH

**Who says it?
Write DUA for Duane,
DON for Donna,
MAN for doorman.**

☐ Can I help you, sir … ma'am?
☐ How much is a room here?
☐ Fifty dollars a night.
☐ No problem.
☐ Where's a phone booth?

 **Watch section 2.**

## AFTER YOU WATCH

**1   Ask and answer these questions.**
How much is a room at the hotel?
How much is a room at a budget hotel?

**2   Fill in the blanks with words from the box.**

| |
|---|
| free |
| moderate |
| numbers |
| friends |
| expensive |

**Donna:**  Hotels. Very expensive, _____ , _____ , ah, budget.
**Duane:**  _____ in New York.
**Duane:**  Telephone _____ .
**Duane:**  _____ rooms.

**SECTION 3   0 2 : 3 4**

*(to Duane: D...U...A...N...E... Yes, yes.)*

## WHILE YOU WATCH

**Write down these things:**

1   The first (Franklin's) phone number.

_____

2   The first word that Duane spells.

_____

3   The second (Marsha's) phone number.

_____

 **Watch section 3.**

## AFTER YOU WATCH

**1   What does Franklin say? There are two choices. Both (A) and (B) are correct answers. Practice with a partner.**

1   You are Duane. Your partner reads the (A) answers.
2   Your partner is Duane. You read the (B) answers.

**Duane:**  Hi, Franklin?
**Franklin:**  (A) Hi.
         (B) Yes.
**Duane:**  How are you doing?
**Franklin:**  (A) OK. Who is this?
         (B) Fine. Who's that?
**Duane:**  It's Duane.
**Franklin:**  (A) Sorry?
         (B) Pardon me?
**Duane:**  Duane.
**Franklin:**  (A) Who?
         (B) Sorry, who are you?
**Duane:**  From Minnesota?
**Franklin:**  (A) How do you spell that?
         (B) Can you spell that?
**Duane:**  M...I...N...E ... How do you spell it?
**Donna:**  Double n. It's double n.
**Duane:**  Oh, it's M...I...double N...E...S...O...T...A
**Franklin:**  (A) No, your name.
         (B) I mean your name.
**Duane:**  Oh, Duane! Right. D...U...A ...
**Franklin:**  (A) Twain?
         (B) 'T'?
**Duane:**  No, D.  D...U...A...N...E.
Franklin? Franklin? Franklin, are you there?

**2   Fill in the blanks in Donna's conversations.**

1
**Donna:**  Hi.
**Person:**  _____
**Donna:**  This is Donna from Minnesota?
**Person:**  _____
**Donna:**  Yeah! Is Marsha there?
**Person:**  _____
**Donna:**  No?

2
**Donna:**  Linda!
**Linda:**  _____
**Donna:**  Hi! It's me.
**Linda:**  _____
**Donna:**  That's right! Donna.
**Linda:**  _____
**Donna:**  I'm in New York ...

**3   Practice the conversations with a partner.**

## SECTION 4  0 4 : 2 3

*(to the end)*

### WHILE YOU WATCH

*Look at these sentences and number them in the order you hear them from 1 to 7.*

- ☐ Wait for us!
- ☐ I don't know.
- ☐ I'm not sure.
- ☐ What do you mean?
- ☐ This is the place.
- ☐ Hey, Donna.
- ☐ Look for Max.

 **Watch section 4.**

### AFTER YOU WATCH

*Check the correct words to complete the sentences.*

**Duane:** This is the (☐ space ☐ place). (☐ There's ☐ Theirs) the lake, and (☐ we are ☐ we're) south of the lake. That's it. (☐ By ☐ Near) the fountain.

**Donna:** (☐ Who ☐ Where) is Max? Is he (☐ of ☐ from) college?

**Duane:** Hey, (☐ Max! ☐ man!)
**Max:** (☐ Say ☐ Hey), man.
**Duane:** (☐ This is ☐ Mrs.) Donna.

**Max:** Hey, Donna. OK, (☐ you guys ☐ you're nice), follow (☐ we ☐ me).

 **Watch the whole story again.**

*Imagine . . .*

**The answers to this section are NOT in the story. Use your imagination.**

**Read this text about Max. Make sentences about Duane and Donna.**

Max is a student at Columbia University in New York City. He's 22, and he's a student of engineering. Max is a great rollerblader! Max isn't from New York. He's from Chicago. Max isn't married, he's single. Max's father is an engineer, and his mother is a dentist. Max's apartment is on the Upper West Side in New York.

# Vocabulary

## Signs

*What do they mean?*
*Write the numbers in the boxes.*

- [ ] Don't smoke here.
- [ ] Don't park your car here.
- [ ] You can turn first left.
      Don't turn second left.
- [ ] You can cross the street.
- [ ] Don't drive in the bus lane.
- [ ] Don't cross the street.

## Phones

*Read the phone instructions.*
*True or false? Check ✓ the*
*boxes.*

|   |   | true | false |
|---|---|:---:|:---:|
| 1 | SOS calls are 25 cents. | ☐ | ☐ |
| 2 | The emergency number is 911. | ☐ | ☐ |
| 3 | A local call is a quarter. | ☐ | ☐ |
| 4 | First deposit a coin, then listen for a tone. | ☐ | ☐ |
| 5 | Don't deposit one-cent coins. | ☐ | ☐ |
| 6 | "Deposit" means "put in." | ☐ | ☐ |

## Hotels

**1  Look at the hotel guide. Fill in the blanks.**

1  The phone number of the Tammany Hotel is _____ .
2  There are _____ rooms in the Shilton Towers.
3  There _____ 24-hour room service at the Tammany
   Hall.
4  There is valet parking at _____ .
5  A single room at the Value Inn is _____ a night.

**2  Fill in the blanks in the conversation.**

**Hotel:**  This is the _____ hotel. Can I _____ ?
**You:**  How _____ ?
**Hotel:**  Single or double?
**You:**  _____
**Hotel:**  _____ dollars.
**You:**  _____ dollars _____ ?
**Hotel:**  No, _____ a night!

**3  Use the hotel guide. Make more conversations in pairs.**

### UPPER MIDTOWN ACCOMODATIONS

**VERY EXPENSIVE**
**Presidential Skyline Plaza** ☎ *075 4000*
Rooms 891 Double $600 Single $450,
5 restaurants, 24-hour room service,
valet parking, business facilities,
concierge floors, indoor pool,
health suite.

**EXPENSIVE**
**Shilton Towers** ☎ *064 4433*
Rooms 1807 Double $350 Single $275,
2 restaurants, coffee shop, 24-hour
room service, parking, business facilities.

**MODERATE**
**Tammany Hotel** ☎ *022 1873*
Rooms 160 Double $120 Single $95,
coffee shop, room service 7 am – 10 pm.

**BUDGET**
**Value Inn** ☎ *199 8263*
Rooms 392 Double $85 Single $50,
coffee shop.

# TELL THE STORY

*Tell the story. Can you make sentences about each picture?*

# Exercises

N

## Exercise 1

*Put* a *or* an *in the blanks.*

1 ___ museum
2 ___ bridge
3 ___ statue
4 ___ river
5 ___ island
6 ___ building
7 ___ avenue
8 ___ airport
9 ___ park

*Find these things on the map.*

## Exercise 2

*Use the map. Practice with a partner.*

A: Harlem. How do you spell that?
B: H – A – R – L – E – M.

## Exercise 3

In New York, **avenues** are from south to north, and **streets** are from east to west. The east to west street is the **cross street**. 5th Avenue is the center of Manhattan Island. Streets are east or west of 5th Avenue.

*Have conversations about these places:*

Guggenheim Museum – 5th Av. / E. 88th St.
Grand Central Terminal – Park Av. / E. 42nd St.
Museum of Modern Art – 5th Av. / W. 53rd St.
Columbia University – Broadway / W. 116th St.
Trump Tower – 5th Av. / E. 57th St.
St. Patrick's Cathedral – 5th Av. / E. 50th St.
General Post Office – 9th Av. / W. 31st St.
United Nations Headquarters – 1st Av. / E. 43rd St.

*E.g.:*
**Cab driver:** Where to?
**You:** The Guggenheim Museum, please.
**Cab driver:** Where's that?
**You:** Fifth Avenue and East Eighty-eighth Street.

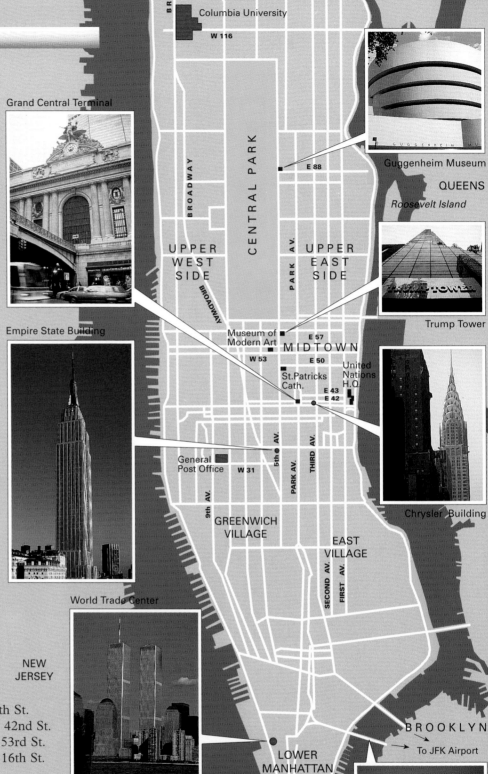

Grand Central Terminal

Guggenheim Museum

Trump Tower

Chrysler Building

Empire State Building

World Trade Center

Statue of Liberty

South Street Seaport

Brooklyn Bridge

# Reference

## Numbers

| 1–10 | 11–20 | 30, 40 … |
|---|---|---|
| one | eleven | twenty-one |
| two | twelve | thirty-two |
| three | thirteen | forty-three |
| four | fourteen | fifty-four |
| five | fifteen | sixty-five |
| six | sixteen | seventy-six |
| seven | seventeen | eighty-seven |
| eight | eighteen | ninety-eight |
| nine | nineteen | ninety-nine |
| ten | twenty | |

```
      100 – one hundred
    1,000 – one thousand
1,000,000 – one million
```

## Ordinal numbers

| 1st | – | first | 6th | – | sixth |
|---|---|---|---|---|---|
| 2nd | – | second | 7th | – | seventh |
| 3rd | – | third | 8th | – | eighth |
| 4th | – | fourth | 9th | – | ninth |
| 5th | – | fifth | 10th | – | tenth |

*then add* **-th, -st, -nd:**
eleventh, twenty-first, thirty-second,
forty-third, fifty-fourth, etc.

## The alphabet

*Say the letters of the alphabet:*

```
B C D E G P T V Z
F L M N S X
A H J K
Q U W
I Y
R
O
```

## a / an indefinite articles

Use **an** *before the sound of a vowel.*
*The vowels are* **a, e, i, o, u.**

an island
an airport
an expensive hotel
an orange
an umbrella

*In these examples,* **u** *has the sound of a
consonant* **y**:
a uniform, a union, a unit

Use **a** *before the sound of a consonant.
The consonants are* **b, c, d, f, g, h, j,
k, l, m, n, p, q, r, s, t, v, w, x, y, z.**

a phone booth
a budget hotel
a park

## The verb *to be*, present tense

AFFIRMATIVE AND NEGATIVE

| I | 'm<br>am<br>'m not<br>am not | from New York.<br>American. |
|---|---|---|
| He<br>She<br>It | 's<br>is<br>isn't<br>is not | |
| We<br>You<br>They | 're<br>are<br>aren't<br>are not | |

QUESTIONS

| Am | I | American?<br>from New York? |
|---|---|---|
| Is | he<br>she<br>it | |
| Are | we<br>you<br>they | |

SHORT ANSWERS

| Yes, I am. / No, I'm not. |
|---|
| Yes, he is. / No, he isn't.<br>Yes, she is. / No, she isn't.<br>Yes, it is. / No, it isn't. |
| Yes, we are. / No, we aren't.<br>Yes, you are. / No, you aren't.<br>Yes, they are. / No, they aren't. |

## Question words

How much is a room here?
Where's a phone booth?
Who is Max?

## Pronouns and possessive adjectives

OBJECT PRONOUNS
It's me. / Follow me.
Can I help you?
Wait for us.

POSSESSIVE ADJECTIVES
This is our first day in New York.
He isn't my friend.

| Subject pronoun | Possessive adjective | Object pronoun |
|---|---|---|
| I | my | me |
| you | your | you |
| he | his | him |
| she | her | her |
| it | its | it |
| we | our | us |
| they | their | them |

## Greetings

| GREETING | RESPONSE |
|---|---|
| Hi. | Hi. |
| Hey. | Hey. |
| Hello. | Hello. |
| How are you doing? | How are you doing? |
| Good morning. | Good morning. |
| Good afternoon. | Good afternoon. |
| Good evening. | Good evening. |

## Expressions

Come on.
Can I help you?
How much is a room here?
This is (Donna).
No problem.
Is (Marsha) there?
That's right.
How do you spell it?
I'm not sure.
I don't know.
What do you mean?
He's a friend of (Michael's).
You guys … (*male, female, or male
and female*)
Follow me.

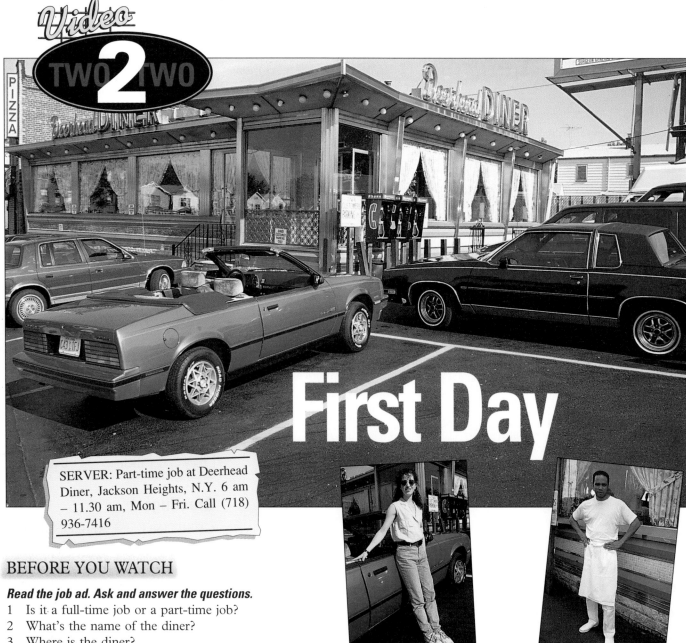

# First Day

SERVER: Part-time job at Deerhead Diner, Jackson Heights, N.Y. 6 am – 11.30 am, Mon – Fri. Call (718) 936-7416

## BEFORE YOU WATCH

*Read the job ad. Ask and answer the questions.*
1  Is it a full-time job or a part-time job?
2  What's the name of the diner?
3  Where is the diner?
4  What does "N.Y." mean?
5  Is the job mornings, afternoons, or evenings?
6  Is the job on weekends?
7  What's the telephone number?

 *Watch First Day.*

## AFTER YOU WATCH

**1  Put the words from the box with the photos.**

| | |
|---|---|
| server | Brandon |
| lawyer | Mr. Winthrop |
| college student | Tammy |
| chef | Ashley |

**2  Ask and answer questions, e.g.:**
Who's the chef?

name: _____
job: _____

name: _____
job: _____

name: _____
job: _____

name: _____
job: _____

## SECTION 1  `00`:`00`

*(from the beginning to **Tammy** ... His name's Brandon.)*

### BEFORE YOU WATCH

**Who says it? Do you remember?**
**Write A for Ashley, T for Tammy.**

- [ ] You're early.
- [ ] This is my first job.
- [ ] Nice to meet you.
- [ ] No, hon. I'm just a server.
- [ ] I'm a psychology major.
- [ ] How is it?
- [ ] His name's Brandon.

### WHILE YOU WATCH

**Are your answers in BEFORE YOU WATCH correct?**

 **Watch section 1 and find out.**

### AFTER YOU WATCH

**1  Answer these questions about Ashley.**
1  What color is her car?
2  Is her car a sedan, or is it a convertible?
3  Is this her first job?
4  What is her major in college?
5  What color is her uniform?

**2  Fill in the blanks with words from the box.**

| are | one | really | way | closet |

**Tammy:** Oh, _____ ? The uniforms _____ in the _____ .
This _____ . Here are the uniforms.  Go ahead and
choose _____ .

## SECTION 2  `01`:`34`

*(to **Brandon**: ... OK. Now you.)*

### BEFORE YOU WATCH

**What do you need for a club sandwich? Check the boxes.**

- [ ] bread
- [ ] bacon
- [ ] tuna
- [ ] onion
- [ ] turkey
- [ ] coleslaw

- [ ] mayonnaise
- [ ] lettuce
- [ ] beef
- [ ] cheese
- [ ] tomatoes
- [ ] peanut butter

### WHILE YOU WATCH

**Are your answers in BEFORE YOU WATCH correct?**

**Watch section 2 and find out.**

### AFTER YOU WATCH

**Fill in the blanks with is or are.**

There _____ some tomatoes.
There _____ some slices of tomato.

There _____ some lettuce.

There _____ some bread.
There _____ some slices of bread.

There _____ some bacon.
There _____ some pieces of bacon.

There _____ some mayonnaise.

There _____ some turkey.
There _____ some pieces of turkey.

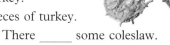

There _____ some coleslaw.
There _____ some cups of coleslaw.

19

WATCHING THE VIDEO

## SECTION 3 `0 3 : 0 0`

*(to **Brandon:** … There's a customer, Ashley. )*

## BEFORE YOU WATCH

***Making a club sandwich: number the pictures in order
from 1 to 9. Then complete these instructions.***

1 First, _____ ,
2 then one _____ .
3 Put some _____ ,
4 then another _____ .
5 Next, some _____ ,
6 and some _____ ,
7 then another _____ ,
8 and some _____ .
9 Finally, _____ .

## WHILE YOU WATCH

1 Play the video, pause, and give Ashley instructions.
2 Play the video <u>without sound</u> , and give Ashley
  instructions. Do not pause the video.

 Watch section 3.

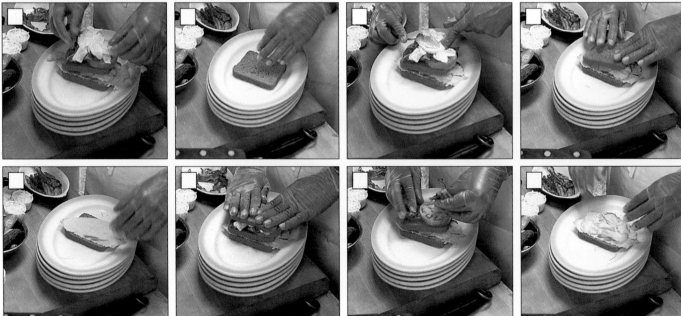

## SECTION 4  `0` `4` : `2` `0`

*(to the end)*

## WHILE YOU WATCH

**Number these sentences from 1 to 6.**

- ☐ Coming right up.
- ☐ Enjoy your meal.
- ☐ I'm your server today.
- ☐ There you go, sir.
- ☐ Good morning, sir.
- ☐ Can I help you?

➡ **Watch section 4.**

## AFTER YOU WATCH

**Write the sentences under the correct pictures.**

- ● That's Harrison Winthrop.
- ● Under here?
- ● Is it in the club sandwich?
- ● What's this?
- ● And what is <u>this</u>?

➡ **Watch the whole story again.**

*Imagine . . .*

**Look at the pictures. What are they thinking? Here are some ideas. Can you think of more?**

Ouch! What's this?
Please don't eat my ring!
He's a great guy, but I can't watch him eat.
Uh, uh. A piece of toothpick.

# Vocabulary

## Food (1)

**1 Write the numbers in the boxes next to the words.**

- ☐ knife
- ☐ bacon
- ☐ lettuce
- ☐ pickles
- ☐ empty cups
- ☐ cutting board
- ☐ parsley
- ☐ plates
- ☐ turkey
- ☐ toothpicks
- ☐ slices of bread
- ☐ tomatoes
- ☐ slices of tomato
- ☐ cups of coleslaw
- ☐ mayonnaise

**2 Which words are NOT in the video dialogue? <u>Underline</u> them.**

## Food (2)

**1 What do you need for a cheeseburger?**
**Read the instructions. Put them in the correct order.**
**Number the instructions from 1 to 9.**

1 _____
2 _____
3 _____
4 _____
5 _____
6 _____
7 _____
8 _____
9 _____

**D** Put some slices of tomato on the cheese,

**C** put some mayonnaise on the bottom half,

**E** then a piece of lettuce.

**B** and some onion rings,

**A** then a slice of cheese.

**F** Finally, put the top half of the bun on top.

**G** then another piece of lettuce.

**H** Next, put the burger on the lettuce,

**I** First, cut the bun in half,

**2 Now write instructions for your favorite food.**

## On the table

**1 Look at the words in the boxes.**

| prepositions |
| --- |
| in  on  under  next to  behind  in front of |

| extra vocabulary |
| --- |
| fries  napkin  check  cola  sugar  salt  pepper<br>Sweet 'N' Low  (bottle of) ketchup  drinking straw<br>knife  fork  spoon  cup  saucer  glass  table |

**2 Write sentences about the picture, e.g.:**
A: There's a spoon in the cup.
B: There are some fries on the plate.
C: There's some cola in the glass.

**3 Look at these examples, then ask and answer questions**
**about the picture.**
A: Is there a spoon in the cup?
B: Are there any fries on the plate?
C: Is there any cola in the glass?

# TELL THE STORY

*Tell the story. Can you make sentences about each picture?*

# Exercises

## Menu

| BEVERAGES | | SANDWICHES | |
|---|---|---|---|
| orange juice - small | 0.85 | special club sandwich | 5.25 |
| orange juice - large | 0.95 | B.L.T. | |
| coffee - our special blend | 0.75 | (bacon, lettuce & tomato) | 3.65 |
| hot chocolate | 0.95 | tuna with mayonnaise | 3.40 |
| tea | 0.80 | ham with Swiss cheese | 4.30 |
| iced tea | 0.85 | | |

**sodas**
(cola, lemon / lime, diet cola)
regular ................. 0.80
large ................... 1.10

**milkshake**
(chocolate, strawberry, vanilla)
regular ................. 1.50
large ................... 1.85

**HOT SANDWICHES**
all served with French fries, cup of
coleslaw and pickle
hamburger ................. 4.50
cheeseburger ............. 4.80
chicken breast & salad .... 5.10
hot pastrami on rye ....... 5.20

## Exercise 1

*Fill in the blanks in this conversation.*

**Server:** Good _____ , _____ . My _____ 's Tammy
and I'm _____ server today. Can I help _____ ?
**Customer:** Special club _____ , and _____ orange
_____ , please.
**Server:** Coming _____ up.
**Customer:** Thank _____ .

**Server:** There you _____ , _____ . Enjoy _____ meal.
**Customer:** Thank you.

## Exercise 2

*Choose a conversation. There are two choices.*
*Both (A) and (B) are correct answers. Practice with a partner.*

**Server:** Good (**A:** morning **B:** afternoon),
(**A:** sir **B:** ma'am).
(**A:** My name's **B:** I'm) Tammy,
and I'm your server.
(**A:** Can **B:** May ) I help you?
**Customer:** (**A:** Yes **B:** Sure), a hamburger
(**A:** and **B:** with) fries, please.
**Server:** (**A:** Anything else? **B:** Anything to drink?)
**Customer:** A diet cola.
**Server:** Regular or large?
**Customer:** (**A:** Regular, please. **B:** Large.)
**Server:** Is that it?
**Customer:** (**A:** Yes, thank you. **B:** Yes, that's it.)

## Exercise 3

*Ask and answer questions about the menu.*

**A:** How much is the ham with Swiss cheese sandwich?
**B:** Four thirty. / Four dollars and thirty cents.

**A:** How much is the regular cola?
**B:** Eighty cents.

## Exercise 4

*Use the menu. Work with a partner and role-play more conversations.*

## Exercise 5

*Fill in the blanks with question words.*

1 _____ 's the knife? It's on the cutting board.
2 _____ is the chef? Brandon is.
3 _____ 's her job? She's the manager.
4 _____ color are the uniforms? They're pink and white.
5 _____ 's that? It's her ring.

## Exercise 6

*Fill in the blanks with* a, an, some, the, *or* any.

1 Is there _____ ketchup? Yes. There you go.
2 He's _____ important lawyer.
3 There's _____ orange juice in the glass.
4 There's _____ piece of parsley on the plate.
5 Is it on _____ counter?

24

# Reference

## There is some ... / There are some ...

| There | is<br>'s | some | bread.<br>turkey. |
| | isn't<br>is not | any | lettuce.<br>water. |
| | are<br>'re | some | sandwiches.<br>slices of bread. |
| | aren't<br>are not | any | pieces of lettuce.<br>glasses.<br>glasses of water. |

| Is<br>Isn't | there | any | bread?<br>turkey? |
| Are<br>Aren't | | | sandwiches?<br>pieces of bread? |

**Note:**
*You cut something into **slices** with a knife.*
*So, you can say **pieces of bread** or **slices of bread**.*

## Countable and uncountable nouns

| **││││││││││││** | ⬛⬛⬛ |
|---|---|
| **countable** | **uncountable** |
| sandwiches | bread |
| tomatoes | mayonnaise |
| glasses | water |
| glasses of water | turkey |
| pieces of turkey | lettuce |
| slices of turkey | juice |

*Some nouns can be countable or*
*uncountable:*

There are some turkeys in the
farmer's field.
*(animals, plural)*

There is some turkey on my plate.
*(meat, singular)*

## Possessive adjectives

my, your, his, her, our, their
*(See page 17 Reference for Duane and*
*Donna in New York.)*

## Prepositions

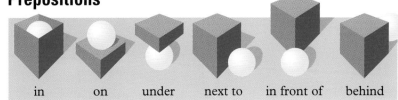

in     on     under     next to     in front of     behind

## Introductions

INFORMAL
A: Hi, I'm (Ashley).
B: Nice to meet you.
A: You too. / And you.

FORMAL
A: Good morning. I'm Harrison Winthrop.
B: Pleased to meet you, Mr. Winthrop.
   I'm Brandon Arnold.

## Forms of address

| formal, strangers | last name | first name | informal |
|---|---|---|---|
| sir<br>madam / ma'am | Mr. Winthrop<br>Ms. Franklin<br>Mrs. Mather<br>Miss Carter | Ashley<br>Brandon | hon (= honey)★ |

*★ "hon," usually from older people to younger people. Very informal. You often hear*
*it from servers in stores and informal restaurants. Understand it, but do not use it.*

## Sequence words

1 First ...
2 Then ... / Next ...
3 Finally ...

## Adjectives

How is it? / What's it like?
How are they? / What are they like?

| It's<br>They're<br>He's<br>She's | fabulous.<br>nice.<br>famous.<br>important. |

It's nice (*singular*). / They're nice
(*plural*).

**Notes:**
He's **very** famous.
He's a **real** important lawyer. / He's
a **really** important lawyer.

*Most grammar books (and British*
*speakers) prefer **really**, but in modern*
*spoken American English, **real** is very*
*frequent. It's informal.*

## Question words

Who is it?
   It's (Ashley).
What is it?
   It's a (toothpick).
Where are they?
   They're (in) (the closet).
What color is it?
   It's (gray).

## Expressions

Uh-huh
Oh, really?
This way.
Go ahead and choose one.
Come and meet (the chef).
Watch me.
Now you.
I'm your server today.
Can I help you?
Coming right up.
You don't know?
There you go.
Enjoy your meal.
Thank you.

# Strange Encounter

**Teacher's note:**
There are five sections. This story is exploited section by section **without** viewing the whole story first.

## BEFORE YOU WATCH

*Look at the picture. Read the three texts.*
*Which text is true, do you think?*

This is a story about auto repairs. The car isn't working. It's an old Cadillac, and there's something wrong with the engine. The owner of the car is wearing a blue Levi's jacket and white pants. We can see the repair person's legs. She's from American Auto Repairs, and she's wearing the American Auto Repairs uniform – silver pants and gold boots.

This is a crime story. The criminal is wearing a superhero costume (as a disguise). The costume is silver with gold boots. The criminal has a gun, and is saying, "Don't move! Put your hands up." The guy in the blue jacket doesn't have a gun. He isn't moving. It's a quiet road and there aren't any other cars around.

This is a science-fiction story. This is a lonely and empty road. There's something wrong with the car. The hood is up. The guy in the blue Levi's jacket is looking at the engine. There's an alien from outer space behind him. The alien is wearing a silver and gold suit. The guy can't see the alien.

 **Watch Strange Encounter, section 1.**

**SECTION 1** `0 0 : 0 0`

*(from the beginning to **Vega**: No.)*

Britanny      Scott      Vega

## WHILE YOU WATCH

***Who says it? Write B for Britanny, S for Scott, V for Vega.***

- [ ] What's wrong?
- [ ] I don't know.
- [ ] There's someone behind you.
- [ ] Pardon me.
- [ ] Come with us.
- [ ] Fasten the belt.
- [ ] We're on vacation.
- [ ] So, you aren't American.

➡ ***Watch section 1 again.***

## AFTER YOU WATCH

**1 Is Vega telling the truth? Yes or no? What do you think?**

| | yes | no |
|---|---|---|
| 1 "I don't have a car." | ☐ | ☐ |
| 2 "The engine is fine." | ☐ | ☐ |
| 3 "I'm a movie star." | ☐ | ☐ |
| 4 "They're shooting the movie in Rockport." | ☐ | ☐ |
| 5 "My home is a long way from here." | ☐ | ☐ |
| 6 "I'm in the United States for a movie." | ☐ | ☐ |

**2 Fill in the blanks in the conversation.**

**Vega:** How _____ you _____? My _____ is Vega.

**Britanny:** Vega? That's a _____ name. _____ are you _____?

## SECTION 2 `03:38`

*(to Vega: You're welcome.)*

## WHILE YOU WATCH

***Number these sentences in the correct order from 1 to 6.***

- [ ] You're welcome.
- [ ] Give me the camera.
- [ ] There you go.
- [ ] Are there any pictures left, Scott?
- [ ] This is Rockport.
- [ ] Vega! Wait!

➡ ***Watch section 2.***

## AFTER YOU WATCH

***Check the correct words to complete the sentences.***

1 Take a picture of ( ☐ this ☐ us ☐ it).

2 Give ( ☐ we ☐ us ☐ me) a big smile.

3 Yeah, ( ☐ there ☐ their ☐ they) are two shots left.

**WATCHING THE VIDEO**

## SECTION 3  04 : 58

*(to **Clerk**: You're welcome.)*

### WHILE YOU WATCH

**Read the questions, and find the answers.**
1  What time is it now?
2  How much is the film?
3  What bill does Scott have?
4  How much is the change?

➡️ **Watch section 3.**

### AFTER YOU WATCH

**1  What does Britanny say?**

**Britanny:** Hey, Scott.
_____
_____

**Scott:** OK. Make that two sets of prints, please.

**Britanny:** And Scott,
_____
_____

**Scott:** OK. Do you have 35-millimeter?

**2  Answer these questions with short answers.**
1  Do Scott and Britanny have any more film?
2  Does the store have 35-millimeter film?
3  Does it have Kodak Gold film?
4  Does Scott have a ten-dollar bill?

## SECTION 4  06 : 14

*(to **Police officer**: … Sorry.)*

### BEFORE YOU WATCH

***What does Vega look like?***
***Describe her.***
***Try to answer these questions.***

How old is she?
How tall is she?
What's she wearing?
What kind of hair does she have?
What's her job?
Where's she from?

➡️ **Watch section 4.**

### AFTER YOU WATCH

**1  Number these sentences in the correct order from 1 to 5.**

☐ Are you kidding?
☐ Pardon me. Officer!
☐ What does she look like?
☐ Look, I don't have time for this, guys.
☐ We're looking for a friend.

**2  Underline the mistakes in Scott and Britanny's descriptions of Vega below. Then correct them.**

**Britanny:** She's tall. About thirteen. Weird looking. She's wearing a white two-piece suit and gold sneakers.

**Scott:** And she has orange hair. She looks kind of tired. Like a movie star.

## SECTION 5 `07:16`
*(to the end)*

## WHILE YOU WATCH

**Number these pictures from 1 to 3.**

 **Watch section 5.**

## AFTER YOU WATCH

*Fill in the blanks in these sentences.*

1  _____ careful, Britanny! _____ fall in.
2  Hey, it's _____ four.
3  OK, show _____ the _____ of Vega.
4  That's _____ ! She's _____ here.
5  What _____ you mean? You _____ have the pictures?
6  See you _____ sometime, someplace.
7  _____ for the ride.

 **Watch the whole story again.**

*Imagine ...*

*Imagine Vega's home. Make sentences about it, e.g.:*

It is (a small planet).
It isn't (near the Earth).
There aren't any (cars).
There are (a lot of airplanes and spaceships).
There isn't (any money).
They have (cities under the ocean).
They don't have (hamburger restaurants).

*Compare your sentences with a partner's. Then role-play Vega and a reporter. The reporter asks questions, e.g.:*

What's your planet's name?
Are there any trees on your planet?
Are there twenty-four hours in a day?
How many days are there in a year?
Is there TV on your planet?
Does your planet have air?
Do people on your planet use money?

WATCHING THE VIDEO

# Vocabulary

## Describing people (1)

*Read this description of the police officer. Look at the bold words. Put them in the correct boxes.*

This is Officer McDonald. He is a tall African American in his forties. He has a mustache. He's wearing a police uniform: a light blue **shirt**, and dark blue **pants**. He's wearing a black leather **belt**, with a **gun in a holster** on his right and a **nightstick** on his left. He's wearing a **tie**, and a **cap**. He has a silver Police Department **badge**, and a metal **nametag** on his shirt.

## Describing people (2)

*Look at the chart. Describe two people from this list.*

- a movie star
- a TV character
- a sports star
- a nice person
- an elderly person
- a friend
- a classmate
- an important person
- a weird person
- a child

| GENERAL He's / She's … | HEIGHT She's … | AGE He's … | HAIR She has … | FACE He has … |
|---|---|---|---|---|
| good looking | tall / big | 31 | strange hair | glasses |
| attractive | average height | young / old | blonde hair | a beard |
| weird | short / small | teenage | brown hair | a mustache |
| average | | about 30 | dark hair | brown eyes |
| | | in (his) 30s | white hair | large eyes |
| | | between 30 and 40 | long hair | a thin mouth |
| | | | short hair | |
| | | | tied-back hair | |

## Photography

**1** Write the numbers next to the words in this list.

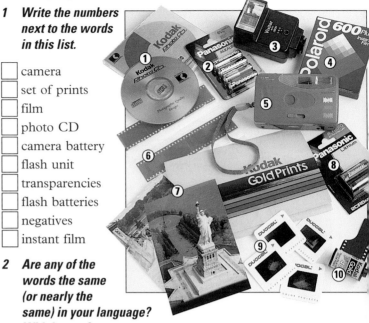

- [ ] camera
- [ ] set of prints
- [ ] film
- [ ] photo CD
- [ ] camera battery
- [ ] flash unit
- [ ] transparencies
- [ ] flash batteries
- [ ] negatives
- [ ] instant film

**2** Are any of the words the same (or nearly the same) in your language? Which ones?

## U.S. money

**U.S. coins**

5¢    1¢    10¢    25¢

*United States and Canadian coins have the same everyday names: "penny" for one cent, "nickel" for five cents, "dime" for ten cents, "quarter" for twenty-five cents. In Canada there is also a one-dollar coin a "loonie" – the bird on the coin is a loon.*

*U.S. bills are all the same color and the same size. Canadian bills are different colors.*

**U.S. bills**

1$

5$

10$

20$

50$

100$

# TELL THE STORY

Tell the story. Can you make sentences about each picture?

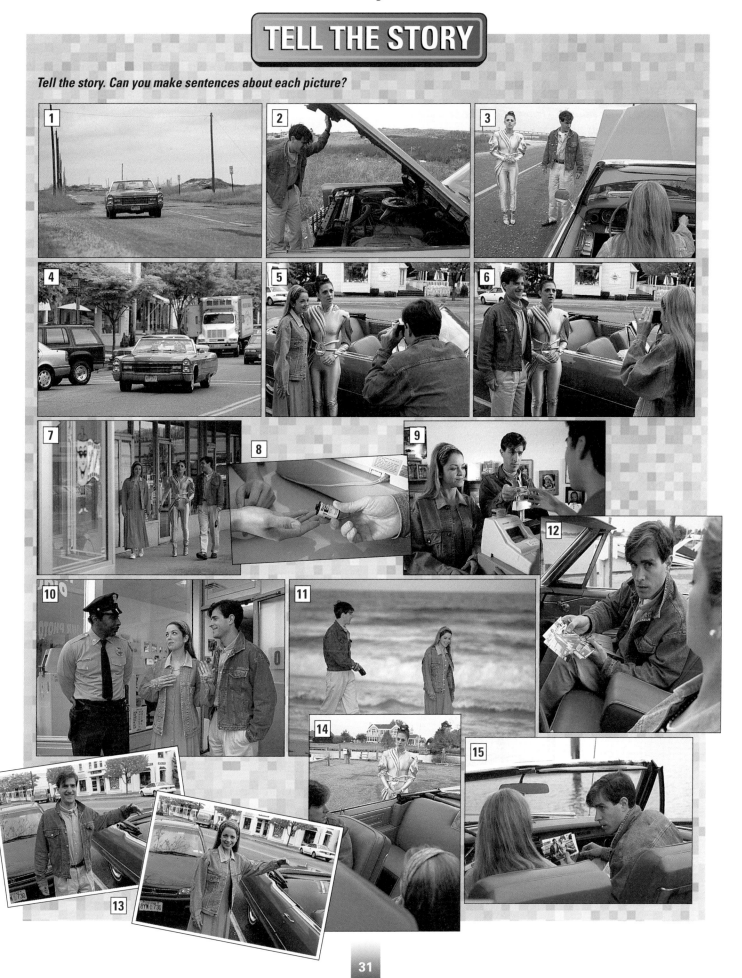

# Exercises

## Exercise 1 *Open conversation*

**YOU are in the photo store. It's two-thirty in the afternoon. Fill in the blanks in this conversation.**

**Clerk:** Good afternoon _____ .

**You:** _____ afternoon. _____ processing, please.

**Clerk:** OK. Ready _____ . OK?

**You:** _____ . Oh, I don't _____ film! Do _____ 35-millimeter?

**Clerk:** Sure. What size? Twenty- _____ or _____ -six exposure?

**You:** _____ .

**Clerk:** What make?

**You:** _____ makes _____ have?

**Clerk:** We _____ Fuji, Kodak and Agfa.

**You:** _____ .

**Clerk:** Four hundred film, two hundred, or one hundred?

**You:** I don't know.

**Clerk:** One hundred ASA is for bright sun. Four hundred _____ indoors and bad light. Two _____ is multi-purpose. It's kind of in the middle.

**You:** OK. _____ .

**Clerk:** OK. There you _____ .

**You:** How _____ ?

**Clerk:** Eight twenty-seven with tax.

**You:** _____ go.

**Clerk:** Out of _____ . That's _____ _____ change.

**You:** _____ .

## Exercise 2

**Work with a partner. How many questions and answers can you make from the words in the boxes? E.g.:**

**A:** Do you have a **comb** in your **pocket**?
**B:** Yes, I do. / No, I don't.

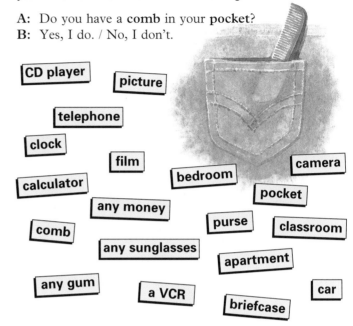

CD player
picture
telephone
clock
film
bedroom
camera
calculator
pocket
any money
purse
classroom
comb
any sunglasses
apartment
any gum
a VCR
briefcase
car

## Exercise 3

**Work with a SECOND partner. Ask about the FIRST partner, e.g.:**

Does (Yoko / Carlos) have a comb in (her / his) pocket?
Yes, (she / he) does. / No, (she / he) doesn't.

## Exercise 4

We're over here!
*Take a picture of us.*

**Continue.**
*Take a picture of ...*
1  Look! The Statue of Liberty's over there!
2  Quick! There's Michael Jackson!
3  Hey, isn't that Princess Diana?
4  Look! Aren't those trees beautiful!
5  Hey! I'm wearing my favorite clothes.

## Exercise 5

**Give these instructions to a partner.**

Come here. Show me your book. Put it on the table. Go to the window. Open it. Be careful! Don't fall out. Close the window. Wait. Get a board marker. Go to the board. Draw a picture. Draw a car. Go ahead! Try it! Come here. Stand on one leg. Give me a smile. Don't laugh! Don't fall over!

**Think of a new set of instructions.**

# Reference

## *Have* present tense

AFFIRMATIVE

| I You We They | have | a camera. a problem. an idea. some pictures. some film. |
|---|---|---|
| She He (It) | has | |

NEGATIVE

| I You We They | don't do not | have | a camera. a problem. an idea. any pictures. any film. |
|---|---|---|---|
| She He (It) | doesn't does not | | |

QUESTIONS AND SHORT ANSWERS

| Do | I you we they | have | a camera? a problem? an idea? any pictures? any film? |
|---|---|---|---|
| Does | she he (it) | | |

Yes, you do. / No, you don't.
Yes, I do. / No, I don't.
Yes, we do. / No, we don't.
Yes, they do. / No, they don't.

Yes, she does. / No, she doesn't.
Yes, he does. / No, he doesn't.
Yes, it does. / No, it doesn't.

## Object pronouns

| Take a picture of Look at Come with Help Listen to | me. her. him. it. us. them. |
|---|---|

| Give Show | me her him it us them | the camera. the pictures. |
|---|---|---|

See you again.

## Imperatives

| AFFIRMATIVE | NEGATIVE |
|---|---|
| Do this. | Don't do that. |
| Push. | Don't pull. |
| Turn the key. | Don't turn the key. |
| Try it again. | Don't try it again. |
| Fasten the belt. | Don't fasten the belt. |
| Be careful! | Don't fall in! |
| Be quiet! | Don't be stupid! |

## Describing people

QUESTIONS
What's she like?
What does she look like?
What do they look like?

Does she have long hair?
Does he have a beard?

What color is her hair?

She is weird. / She looks weird.
She looks like an alien.

## Present continuous tense

They're shooting the movie in Rockport.
We're looking for a friend.
She's wearing a silver one-piece suit.
Are you kidding?

*BE* + VERB *-ING* FORM
AFFIRMATIVE AND NEGATIVE

| I | 'm 'm not | wearing | a silver suit. glasses. jeans. gold boots. |
|---|---|---|---|
| He She | 's isn't | | |
| We You They | 're aren't | | |

QUESTIONS

| Am | I | wearing | a silver suit? glasses? jeans? gold boots? |
|---|---|---|---|
| Is | he she | | |
| Are | we you they | | |

SHORT ANSWERS
Yes, I am. / No, I'm not.
Yes, (he) is. / No, (she) isn't.
Yes, (we) are. / No, (they) aren't.

## Asking about prices

How much is it? / How much is a film?
How much are they? / How much are films?

It's $7.95. / They're $7.95 each.
(seven dollars and ninety-five cents / seven ninety-five)

## Expressions

What's wrong?
Pardon me.
Go ahead.
How do you do?
You're welcome.
Ready at (4 o'clock), OK?
Make that (two sets of prints).
Out of (twenty).
(She looks) kind of (weird).
Are you kidding?
What do you mean?
See you again …

# Video

## 4

Big Deal!

Lauren    Tony    Kevin / James    Stephanie    Frankie

## BEFORE YOU WATCH

**1  Describe these people. Try to answer the questions.
You can use the words in the box.**

> sunglasses   earrings   mustache   T-shirt   gold chain
> long hair   short hair   curly hair   make-up   lipstick

What ('s) (he) wearing?
How old (are) (they)?
What color's (her) hair?
(Are) (they) rich? / poor?
What (are) (their) jobs, do you think?

**2  Describe the car.**
What color is it?
What make is it? Do you know?
Where's it from?
Is it fast? / expensive? / modern?

**3  Answer these questions.**
Which one is "the boss"?
Whose car is it, do you think?
Would you like this car?
Whose house is it, do you think?
Would you like this house?

  **Watch Big Deal.**

## AFTER YOU WATCH

**True or false? Check the boxes.**

| | | true | false |
|---|---|---|---|
| 1 | James and Kevin are police officers. | ☐ | ☐ |
| 2 | Mr. Vidal has a daughter. | ☐ | ☐ |
| 3 | Mr. Vidal's dog is friendly. | ☐ | ☐ |
| 4 | Lauren is Mr. Vidal's personal assistant. | ☐ | ☐ |
| 5 | Frankie is one of Mr. Vidal's business associates. | ☐ | ☐ |
| 6 | Mr. Olsen is James and Kevin's boss. | ☐ | ☐ |

## SECTION 1 `0` `0` : `0` `0`

*(from the beginning to the sign "Go ahead ...")*

### WHILE YOU WATCH

**Watch James and Kevin. Mark their route to the door. Listen to Stephanie. Mark their route to the pool.**

 **Watch section 1.**

### AFTER YOU WATCH

**1   Mr. Vidal has a guard dog. There is a warning sign about the dog.**
What are the words on the sign?

**2   Work with a partner. What do you remember about James and Kevin? Student A asks questions 1 to 4. Student B asks questions 5 to 8. Don't look at the pictures!**

1   Which one's wearing a black T-shirt?
2   Which one's wearing a brown belt?
3   Which one's wearing white sneakers?
4   Which one's wearing a jacket?

5   Which one's wearing a gray T-shirt?
6   Which one's wearing a black belt?
7   Which one's wearing black shoes?
8   Which one's wearing a watch?

### AFTER YOU WATCH

**1   Tony gives Lauren some instructions at the beginning. What are they?**
Call …
Get …
Cancel …

**2   Tony gives Lauren the dog leash. What is his instruction?**
Take …

**3   What are Mr. Olsen's instructions to James and Kevin?**
First …
Then …

## SECTION 2 `0` `1` : `2` `2`

*(to **James:** … and sixty for you.)*

### BEFORE YOU WATCH

**Match these sentences to the pictures. Write the number of the sentence in the box on the picture.**

1   Same time next week, huh?
2   First-class merchandise.
3   Don't forget, call Mr. Olsen this afternoon.
4   See you by the pool in one hour.
5   OK, guys. Right this way.
6   Frankie, the suit!

 **Watch section 2.**

WATCHING THE VIDEO

## SECTION 3 `0 3 : 3 4`

*(to Tony: ... And coffee.)*

## WHILE YOU WATCH (1)

**Listen to Tony on the phone and stop the tape. What does Mr. Olsen say?**

 **Watch section 3.**

**There are two choices. Both (A) and (B) are correct answers. Practice with a partner.**

1 You are Tony. Your partner reads the (A) answers
2 Your partner is Tony. You read the (B) answers.

Olsen: (A) Are James and Kevin with you?
       (B) Are my guys there?
Tony: They're here right now.
Olsen: (A) It's 120 computers, right?
       (B) And they have the computers.
Tony: So, what about my money, Olsen?
Olsen: (A) I'd like the computers first.
       (B) Are you kidding? The computers first, Vidal.
Tony: Yeah, sure, sure.
Olsen: (A) Do you understand?
       (B) Those are my rules of business.
Tony: I know that.

## WHILE YOU WATCH (2)

**What would Tony like for lunch? Check the boxes.**

☐ Chef's salad     ☐ Thousand Island dressing
☐ Caesar salad     ☐ T-bone steak
☐ salad niçoise     ☐ French fries
☐ Waldorf salad     ☐ chocolate ice cream
☐ Russian salad     ☐ strawberry ice cream
☐ olives     ☐ vanilla ice cream
☐ French dressing     ☐ coffee

 **Watch section 3 again.**

## AFTER YOU WATCH

**1 Make questions and answers, e.g.:**
A: Would he like French fries?
B: Yes, he would. / No, he wouldn't.

**2 This is Tony's lunch. Put the correct words in the boxes.**

# SECTION 4 0 5 : 2 1

*(to the end)*

## BEFORE YOU WATCH

**What do you think?**

**Which of these things is James saying? Find the sentence.**

| Do | you like to | can | the cash? |
| Would | | count | it now? |
| Could | | have | |

**Which of these things is Kevin saying? Find the sentence.**

| Could | he | drink | some water? |
| Can't | we | have | a quarter? |
| Would | me | date | your daughter? |

**Which of these things is Tony saying? Find the sentences.**

| No, | wait | in a | rocks. |
| Go | stay | in the | bucks. |
| So | play | with the | truck. |

| This | is | a | rest room! |
| It | isn't | the | restaurant! |

| They're | sort of | in the | fool! |
| There's | water | in a | pool! |
| Theirs | daughter | is a | rule! |

 **Watch section 4.**

## AFTER YOU WATCH

**Answer these questions.**

1 Who has the money?
2 Who's having lunch?
3 Who'd like some water?
4 Who has another appointment?
5 Who can't swim?
6 Is she telling the truth, do you think?

**Watch the whole story again.**

*Imagine* ...

**Here are some questions. The answers are not in the video. Use your imagination. Try to answer them.**

1 How much money is there in the briefcase?
2 Are the computers "first-class merchandise"?
3 Does Frankie know about the computers?
4 What kind of dog is it? A German shepherd? A Rottweiler? A Pit bull? Something else?
5 Is the dog really dangerous?
6 Does Stephanie have any brothers or sisters?
7 Whose car is the Ferrari? Is it Tony's or Stephanie's?
8 Can Tony swim?
9 Is Lauren on a diet?
10 Are James and Kevin brothers?

**Can you think of any more questions? Ask them.**

# Vocabulary

## House and pool

*Write the numbers next to the correct words below.*

front yard

backyard

| | | | |
|---|---|---|---|
| ☐ gate | ☐ planter |
| ☐ pool | ☐ lawn |
| ☐ chair | ☐ pool steps |
| ☐ sports car | ☐ trees |
| ☐ wall | ☐ bar |
| ☐ cart | ☐ panel truck |
| ☐ bushes | ☐ patio |
| ☐ driveway | ☐ garage |
| ☐ table | ☐ gazebo / summerhouse |
| ☐ barbecue | ☐ umbrella |

## Salads and salad dressings

*Salads are very popular in America. This is a list of popular salads. Use your dictionary and read it.*

"Russian dressing is unknown to the Russians, as is the American variety of French dressing to the French." (Bill Bryson, *Made in America* 1994)

*In America, salad dressings are often "from a bottle." The popular dressings are French, Italian, Thousand Island, and Blue Cheese. You can also ask for "oil and vinegar." Try them!*

## Nationalities in American words

*The names of nationalities, countries, and cities begin with a capital letter:*
Parmesan cheese, French onion soup

*How many of these examples do you know? Match the name with the place.*

| | |
|---|---|
| Neapolitan ice cream | France |
| Spanish omelette | Vienna, Austria |
| Parmesan cheese | Hamburg, Germany★ |
| Canadian bacon | Greece |
| French fries | Spain |
| Danish pastries | Parma, Italy |
| Hamburger steak | England |
| Spaghetti Bolognese | Switzerland |
| Swiss cheese | Bologna, Italy |
| Viennese coffee | Denmark |
| English breakfast tea | Canada |
| Greek salad | Naples, Italy |

celery     walnuts     (French) green beans     anchovies

| salad | Where does the name come from? | What are the ingredients? |
|---|---|---|
| CHEF'S SALAD | The Chef's choice. It's a large salad with meat, cheese, and egg. | Chicken or turkey, ham, cheese, eggs, lettuce, tomato |
| WALDORF SALAD | The Waldorf-Astoria Hotel in New York City sometime in the 1890s. | apples, celery, walnuts, mayonnaise |
| SALAD NIÇOISE | The French city, Nice. "Niçoise" means "from Nice." In French, the "C" has an accent, "ç". On many American menus there is no accent: "nicoise." | tuna, green beans, eggs, lettuce, olives, anchovies, potatoes, tomatoes BUT many "tuna and lettuce" salads are called "niçoise" on menus. |
| CAESAR SALAD | Not from Julius Caesar, but from Caesar Cardini, an Italian-American chef in Tijuana, Mexico, in the 1920s. | lettuce, Parmesan cheese, croutons (small pieces of fried bread or toast), garlic dressing |
| RUSSIAN SALAD | Not from Russia, but from a French salad, *Salade russe* (which means Russian salad). | potatoes, carrots, peas, ham, onion, rutabaga or turnip, mayonnaise |

croutons     rutabaga     turnip     garlic     peas

★ Or from the town of Hamburg, New York State. "Hamburg steak" was on New York menus in the 1830s, but unknown in Germany at that time.

# TELL THE STORY

1   **Work with a partner. Number the pictures in the correct order from 1 to 15. Ask questions,** *e.g.:* Which one's first? That one's first. It's outside the house.

2   *Then tell the story. Make sentences about each picture.*

GO AHEAD!

MAKE HIS DAY

# Exercises

## Exercise 1

*Mr. Olsen is selling the computers. Fill in the blanks in this telephone conversation.*

**Mr. Olsen:** Hello? Is this Ms. Jones?

**Ms. Jones:** _____

**Mr. Olsen:** Peter Olsen here.

**Ms. Jones:** Oh, hi there. How _____?

**Mr. Olsen:** Fine, thanks. Uh, I _____ some _____ for sale. Are _____ interested?

**Ms. Jones:** Computers, huh? What make_____?

**Mr. Olsen:** Acme.

**Ms. Jones:** Acme? I don't _____ them.

**Mr. Olsen:** They're first-class _____. Believe me.

**Ms. Jones:** Sure, sure.

**Mr. Olsen:** They're _____ megabyte RAM, one gigabyte _____ disk.

**Ms. Jones:** OK. How _____ do you _____?

**Mr. Olsen:** 120.

**Ms. Jones:** And how _____ are they?

**Mr. Olsen:** _____ dollars each.

**Ms. Jones:** OK, _____ ten. Wait! Who _____ they from?

**Mr. Olsen:** Tony Vidal.

**Ms. Jones:** You're kidding! Forget it!

## Exercise 2

*What is there on the bar? Look at the picture for five seconds. Close the book and write a list from memory.*

## Exercise 3

*James and Kevin are meeting Mr. Vidal at the country club. They're meeting by the statue. Here's a map. Write instructions for them.*

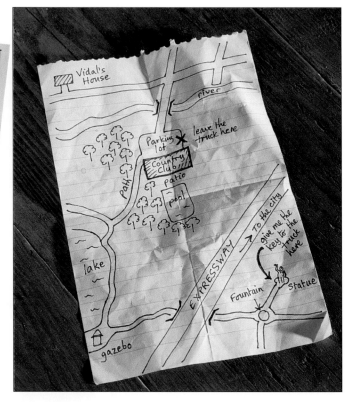

## Exercise 4

*What would you like for your birthday? Write a list of five things. Ask questions about your partner's list, e.g.:*

Would you like a CD?
Which CD would you like?
Would you like a camera?
What kind of camera would you like?

## Exercise 5

*Fill in the blanks on this menu.*

*Then role-play conversations with a partner. Ask about your partner's menu, e.g.:*

A: Hello. Can I help you?
B: Yes, I'd like …
A: Which (flavor) …?
B: Which (flavors) …?
A: I have …
B: I'd …
A: There …
B: How much …?
A: …

*Ice cream* – four flavors!

❀ ............................... $ . ¢.
❀ ............................... $ . ¢.
❀ ............................... $ . ¢.
❀ ............................... $ . ¢.

*Sodas* – three flavors!

❀ ............................... $ . ¢.
❀ ............................... $ . ¢.
❀ ............................... $ . ¢.

*Fruit juice* – three flavors!

❀ ............................... $ . ¢.
❀ ............................... $ . ¢.
❀ ............................... $ . ¢.

# Reference

## Would like

AFFIRMATIVE AND NEGATIVE

| I | 'd | like | a coffee. |
|---|---|---|---|
| You | would | | that one. |
| She | wouldn't | | vanilla. |
| He | | | a salad. |
| We | | | |
| They | | | |

QUESTIONS AND SHORT ANSWERS

| Would | I | like | a coffee? | Yes, I would. / No, I wouldn't. |
|---|---|---|---|---|
| | you | | a salad? | Yes, you would. / No, you wouldn't. |
| | she | | that one? | Yes, she would. / No, she wouldn't. |
| | he | | vanilla? | Yes, he would. / No, he wouldn't. |
| | we | | | Yes, we would. / No, we wouldn't. |
| | they | | | Yes, they would. / No, they wouldn't. |

What would you like?

## Giving directions

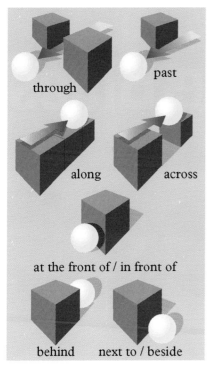

through    past    along    across

at the front of / in front of

behind    next to / beside

It's (right) this way.
It's over there.

| Go | around | the house. |
|---|---|---|
| Take the path | by | |
| | past | |
| | next to | |
| | behind | |
| | in front of | |

| Go | through | the trees. |
|---|---|---|
| Take the path | past | |

| Go | along | the road. |
|---|---|---|
| | across | |

**Note:**
*In American English, we often use **right** with directions:*
It's right this way.
It's right in front of you.

## Review – *have*

*See Reference page 33.*

## Review – sequence words

*See Reference page 25.*

## Possessive pronouns – *Whose?*

Whose is it? / Whose are they?

| Possessive adjective | Possessive pronoun |
|---|---|
| It's my car. | It's mine. |
| It's your pen. | It's yours. |
| They're his kids. | They're his. |
| That's her house. | It's hers. |
| It's our classroom. | It's ours. |
| Those are their bags. | They're theirs. |
| That's its leash. | *(no pronoun)* |

It's Maria's camera. / It's Maria's.
They're Carlos's books. / They're Carlos's.

## Requests

| Could | I | have | some water? |
|---|---|---|---|
| Can | he | | a salad? |
| May | she | | |
| | we | | |
| | they | | |

I'd like some water.
Some water, please.

## Which?

Which one / ones would you like?
Which color would you like?
Which flavor would you like?

This one, please.
These ones, please.
The red one, please.
The small ones, please.
Which one's yours? That one's mine.

## Expressions

Is (Mr. Vidal) at home?
It's that way. / Right this way.
Don't forget …
That's all.
Same time (next week).
OK, guys.
See you (by the pool).
… you understand.
Come on.
What about (my money / your diet)?
Go wait (in the truck).
We're real thirsty. *(See note on page 25.)*

# Video FIVE 5 FIVE

# Office Blues

## BEFORE YOU WATCH

**1** *Look at these pictures of Laura and try to answer these questions.*

PICTURE C
Is she at the office or is she at home?
Is she working?
Is she working in the other pictures?

PICTURE B
She's wrapping a present for someone. Who is it for?
Which of these things can you see in front of her?

*Check the boxes.*

| | | | |
|---|---|---|---|
| ☐ | a pair of scissors | ☐ | a calculator |
| ☐ | wrapping paper | ☐ | a birthday card |
| ☐ | an envelope | ☐ | a key |
| ☐ | some ribbon | ☐ | some Scotch tape |
| ☐ | a pen | ☐ | an audio tape |
| ☐ | a bow | | |

PICTURE D
What is she doing with the gift?

PICTURE A
Who's calling her?

**2** *Can you guess the correct order of the pictures? Write the letters in the boxes below.*

| 1 | | 2 | | 3 | | 4 | |
|---|---|---|---|---|---|---|---|

➡ *Watch Office Blues.*

## AFTER YOU WATCH

*Fill in the blanks.*

Today is a special day for Bruno.
It's his _____ . He's _____
years old. He's wearing a new _____ . It's a birthday
_____ . His mother and father are visiting him in
_____ for his birthday.

## SECTION 1  `0 0 : 0 0`

*(from the beginning to **Olivia**: Good.)*

### BEFORE YOU WATCH

**Who says it? Write B for Bruno, S for Samuel, L for Laura or R for Ms. Revere.**

- [ ] Don't say anything!
- [ ] How are you doing?
- [ ] Can I come in?
- [ ] She's waiting for you, Bruno.
- [ ] That's a great tie!
- [ ] Can you begin right now?
- [ ] Do you have a problem with that?
- [ ] No problem.

 **Watch section 1.**

### AFTER YOU WATCH

**Ask and answer these questions.**

What is Bruno carrying at the beginning?
Which floor is the office on?
Who is looking for Bruno?
Is Bruno busy?
Why is he busy?
Who is Ms. Revere waiting for?
Who is wearing a new tie?
Why is he wearing a new tie?
Who does Ms. Revere have some work for?
When would she like the reports?
Would you like Bruno's job?

## SECTION 2  `0 2 : 0 9`

*(to **Samuel**: Sure. You can finish before five.)*

### BEFORE YOU WATCH

**Fill in the blanks in these two summaries.**

Bruno _____ a problem. He has a lot of _____ and _____ feeling worried and negative. He's _____ to meet his parents at _____ o'clock, so he can't _____ late.

Samuel is very positive. He thinks Bruno _____ do it. It _____ only two-thirty, so he has two and a _____ hours. He can finish _____ five.

 **Watch section 2.**

### AFTER YOU WATCH

**1  Ask and answer these questions.**

Can Bruno stay late tonight?
Why can't he stay late?
Where are Bruno's parents?
How long are they staying there?
When is Bruno going to meet them?
Are they going to see a show or see a movie?
Are they going to have dinner before or after that?

**2  "Going to" often sounds like "gonna." Listen to the section again. Write "going to" or "gonna" after Bruno's sentences.**

| sentence | sound |
|---|---|
| I'm not going to finish it today. | _____ |
| I'm going to meet them tonight. | _____ |
| They're going to be here at five o'clock. | _____ |
| We're going to have dinner. | _____ , |

## SECTION 3  0 2 : 4 8

*(to **Laura**: … be here soon.)*

## BEFORE YOU WATCH

**Number these sentences in the correct order from 1 to 7.**

- [ ] You can't use the copier.
- [ ] No, no, you can't fix it.
- [ ] Are you using it? I can wait.
- [ ] Maybe I can fix it.
- [ ] What's wrong with it?
- [ ] I don't know. I'm waiting for the repair person.
- [ ] It isn't working.

## WHILE YOU WATCH

**When people are not telling the truth, they often don't have "eye contact," they don't "look you in the eye." Watch Laura's eyes. Check the boxes.**

- [ ] She looks up.
- [ ] She looks away.
- [ ] She looks down.
- [ ] She looks to the side.
- [ ] She looks behind her.

 **Watch section 3.**

## AFTER YOU WATCH

**1   What is Laura saying? Find the sentence.**

| Bruno! Oh, no! Uh. So! | What | a are for | you | do using doing | for? here? now? |
|---|---|---|---|---|---|

**What does it sound like? Say it aloud.**

**2   Look at Laura's sentences.**

**I don't know**. I'm waiting for the repair person.

**Does this sound like "I don't know" or "I dunno"?**

The repair person's **going to** be here soon.

**Does this sound like "going to" or "gonna"?**

**3   Choose the correct words.**

1  You can't
   - [ ] using
   - [ ] use
   - [ ] to use
   the copier.

2  I'm not
   - [ ] using
   - [ ] use
   - [ ] to use
   it.

3  The repair person's going
   - [ ] to be
   - [ ] be
   - [ ] being
   here soon.

## SECTION 4 `03:35`

*(to the end)*

## BEFORE YOU WATCH

**Write the sentences under the correct pictures.**

- No, don't do that!
- Bruno, what about my reports?
- I'm going to call my mom and dad.
- Relax, Bruno. I'm kidding!
- I can't wait.
- Sure, I'm going to tell him right now.

 **Watch section 4.**

## AFTER YOU WATCH

**1  Laura is calling Samuel. What is she saying? There are two choices. Both (A) and (B) are correct answers. Practice with a partner.**

1  You are Samuel. Your partner reads the (A) answers.
2  Your partner is Samuel. You read the (B) answers.

**Samuel:** Yes?
**Laura:** (A) Can I speak to Samuel?
(B) Is that you, Samuel?
**Samuel:** Uh, this is Samuel speaking. Who is this?
**Laura:** (A) It's me. Bruno can come now.
(B) It's Laura. We're ready.
**Samuel:** Oh, right.
**Laura:** (A) Is that OK?
(B) Is he with you?
**Samuel:** Sure, I'm going to tell him right now.
**Laura:** (A) See you.
(B) Great.
**Samuel:** Thanks.

**2  Does Ms. Revere have a sense of humor? What do you think?**

 **Watch the whole story again.**

*Imagine . . .*

**What are Bruno's plans for this evening? What's going to happen? What do YOU think?**

1  His parents are going to take him to:
- [ ] a fast-food restaurant
- [ ] The Hard Rock Café
- [ ] the theater restaurant

2  They're going to go there:
- [ ] in a taxi
- [ ] on the subway
- [ ] in his parents' car

3  They're going to see:
- [ ] a musical
- [ ] a comedy
- [ ] a serious drama

4  After the show, they're going to go to:
- [ ] Bruno's apartment
- [ ] his parents' hotel
- [ ] a nightclub

5  They're going to drink:
- [ ] champagne
- [ ] coffee
- [ ] cola

# Vocabulary

## Office equipment

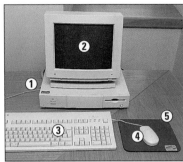

**1**  Look at the pictures above. Write the numbers next to the correct words below.

| | | | |
|---|---|---|---|
| ☐ | desk | ☐ | printer |
| ☐ | stapler | ☐ | calendar |
| ☐ | bulletin board | ☐ | Scotch tape |
| ☐ | drawers | ☐ | adding machine |
| ☐ | PC (personal computer) | ☐ | out box |
| ☐ | mouse | ☐ | mouse pad |
| ☐ | correction fluid | ☐ | fax machine |
| ☐ | Yellow Pages | ☐ | monitor |
| ☐ | keyboard | ☐ | folders |

**2**  Are any of these words the same (or nearly the same) in your language? Which ones?

**3**  You can't remember all the new vocabulary in English. Look at the list, and choose ten of the eighteen words that you want to remember.

## Parties

**1**  This is Bruno's birthday party. His mom and dad are there with his coworkers. Which ones are his mom and dad?

**2**  Look at the picture and read the text.

This is a birthday party. Everyone is wearing a blue **party hat**. There are **decorations** in the copy room. The **balloons** are green and yellow, and there are **streamers**. The streamers are pink, blue, yellow, red and green. Bruno's **birthday cake** has twenty-one **candles**. The cake has white and pink **icing**. Laura's holding Bruno's **present**. It's in pink **wrapping paper**. They're all singing "Happy Birthday." In the small picture, Bruno is **blowing out** the candles. In America, you make a **wish** when you blow out the candles.

**3**  Do you understand all the words in bold now?

**4**  Can you describe the people at the party?

# TELL THE STORY

**Tell the story. Make sentences about each picture.**
**Try to answer these questions.**
What's happening in the picture?
What's going to happen next?

***E.g.:*** Picture 1
Bruno's carrying two heavy cartons.
The doors are going to close.
The elevator's going to go to the 9th floor.

# Exercises

## Exercise 1

**This is Olivia Revere's appointment book for next week. Make sentences about her week with** going to (do), **e.g.:**

(Friday)
She's going to be in Toronto on Friday.
She's going to give a video presentation at a conference.
She's going to be at the conference dinner in the evening.

## Exercise 2

**Match the sentences in column A with the responses in column B.**

| Column A | Column B |
|---|---|
| 1 Can I use your phone? | A Thank you. |
| 2 How are you doing? | B You're welcome. |
| 3 Can you do that before lunch? | C Fine, thanks. |
| 4 It's my birthday today. | D Sure. Go ahead. |
| 5 Thanks for your help. | E Sure. No problem. |
| 6 That's a fabulous tie. | F Congratulations! |

### Appointment book

Monday May 30th
MEMORIAL DAY: PUBLIC HOLIDAY
(staying at the cottage in Westhampton)
Drive back to the city at 4 p.m. (675-3209)
Call Marc – cancel Wednesday evening

Tuesday May 31st
Jogging with Mary-Ann
Lunch meeting – Bill and Sue
Hairdresser – evening

Wednesday June 1st
Meet Marc p.m.
Computer demonstration – 8.45
Plaza Hotel, 5th Av.
(take Samuel and Laura)

Thursday June 2nd
Lunch – Barbara Zawinul
p.m. – to airport 3.30 check-in
Air Canada – Toronto
Stay: Four Seasons Hotel

Friday June 3rd
Data Analysis Conference
Toronto
Give video presentation
8 p.m. Conference dinner

Saturday June 4th
7.30 a.m. check-in –
Air Canada
p.m. – go into office
Aerobics class – 6.30

Sunday June 5th
No appointments!
GET UP LATE!

NOTES

## Exercise 3: Reading for information

**Look at the extract from the Yellow Pages and find the information below. You do not need to read or understand everything.**

- the phone number for Quotation Printing & Stationery
- the phone number for Printers Inc.
- the address of the Fast Copy Midtown office
- the street number for Q.X.X. Repro.
- the place for business cards
- the place for photo CD
- an expression that means "very quick service"

**INSTANT COPY**
- XEROX COPYING
- COLOR COPYING
- LASER PRINTING
- MACINTOSH & IBM OUTPUT & IMAGING
- FREE PICK-UP & DELIVERY SERVICE
- RUSH SERVICE

East 34th St ☎ 619-0344
West 62nd St ☎ 787-0344

**Copying & Duplicating Services** (Cont'd)
Printers Inc.
431 Madison Avenue ... 755-0991
Print Quick Inc.
211 Lexington Avenue .. 947-0893
Quality Copies Services
160 & 44th ........... 950-0317
QUEST WEST SIDE COPIES
Broadway & 81st ...... 787-0445
Quotation Printing & Stationery
112 E 63rd ........... 838-021

Q.X.X. REPRO INC
COMPUTER OUTPUT
CANON COLOR LASER - XEROX
522 Broadway      925-0846

Raddison Duplicating
17 Church Street      571-0626

**FASTCOPY**
"No job is too big, no job is too small"
color copying • one hour photo • digital imaging • MAC/IBM • copies and slides
business cards • free pick-up and delivery • rush service • high and low volume
- **CANON COLOR LASER COPIES • KODAK PHOTO CD**

DOWNTOWN | MIDTOWN | UPPER EAST SIDE | SEAPORT
21 Battery Place | 119 East 50th St | 1280 Madison Ave | 57 Front Street
☎ 285-0614 | ☎ 755-8397 | ☎ 860-0543 | ☎ 385-0716

# Reference

## Can / can't for ability and permission

AFFIRMATIVE AND NEGATIVE

| I | can | do it. |
|---|---|---|
| You | can't | be there. |
| He | cannot | use the copier. |
| She | | sing. |
| We | | |
| They | | |

QUESTIONS AND SHORT ANSWERS

| Can | I | do it? |
|---|---|---|
| Can't | you | be there? |
| | he | use the copier? |
| | she | sing? |
| | we | |
| | they | |

| |
|---|
| Yes, I can. / No, I can't. |
| Yes, you can. / No, you can't. |
| Yes, he can. / No, he can't. |
| Yes, she can. / No, she can't. |
| Yes, we can. / No, we can't. |
| Yes, they can. / No, they can't. |

## Present continuous tense

*BE* + VERB *-ING* FORM
*See also page 33.*

| I | am | listening. |
|---|---|---|
| | 'm | waiting. |
| | 'm not | doing it. |
| She | is | copying the reports. |
| He | 's | taking notes. |
| (It) | isn't | fixing it. |
| | 's not | |
| We | are | |
| You | 're | |
| They | aren't | |
| | 're not | |

QUESTIONS AND SHORT ANSWERS

| Am | I | doing it? |
|---|---|---|
| Is | she | waiting? |
| | he | listening? |
| | | copying the reports? |
| Are | we | fixing it? |
| | she | |
| | he | |

| |
|---|
| Yes, I am. / No, I'm not. |
| Yes, she is. / No, she isn't. |
| Yes, he is. / No, he isn't. |
| Yes, we are. / No, we aren't. |
| Yes, you are. / No, you aren't. |
| Yes, they are. / No, they aren't. |

## Contractions in speech

*Many words are contracted. Auxiliary verbs are often more frequent in the contracted form than the full form, e.g.:*
*'m / 's / isn't / aren't / don't / doesn't / 've / haven't / hasn't / can't / 'd*

*We write these contractions.*

*There are some other contractions that we do not write, but that you need to understand.*
How "ya doin"? = How are you doing?
We're "gonna" have dinner = We're going to have dinner.

*Other frequent examples are:*
"wanna" = want to
"gotta" = got to
"doncha" = don't you
"dunno" = don't know
"gimmee" = give me

*Understand them; say them; but don't write them!*

## Going to future

*BE* + *GOING TO* + VERB
**Affirmative and negative**

| I | 'm | going to | do it | tomorrow. |
|---|---|---|---|---|
| | 'm not | | be there | next week. |
| | | | see him | next year. |
| He | is | | | at 7:30. |
| She | 's | | | on Monday. |
| It | isn't | | | in July. |
| We | are | | | tonight |
| You | 're | | | soon. |
| They | aren't | | | |

QUESTIONS
Am I going to do it?
Is she going to be here tonight?
Are they going to see him tomorrow?

## Time words

I'm going right now.
Can you begin right now?
They're fixing the copier right now.
I'm going to tell him right now.
Can you stay late tonight?
She wants copies this afternoon.
I'd like them before five o'clock.
You can finish before five.
They're in New York for three days.
The repair person's going to be here
  soon.

## Expressions

How are you doing?
No problem.
So?
Not really.
Congratulations!
You see …
You think so?
Maybe …
Sure.
I'm kidding!

# Video SIX **6** SIX

# The Websters

## BREAKFAST HABITS

**1** What time do you get up in the mornings?
- ☐ before seven
- ☐ between seven and eight
- ☐ after eight

**2** Where do you usually have breakfast?
- ☐ at home
- ☐ at work / school
- ☐ in a café / bar / diner

**3** What do you have for breakfast?
- ☐ hot food
- ☐ cold food
- ☐ just a drink

**4** Do you usually have your breakfast ...
- ☐ alone?
- ☐ with your family?
- ☐ with friends / coworkers?

**5** Are you bad-tempered in the mornings?
- ☐ never
- ☐ sometimes
- ☐ always

## BEFORE YOU WATCH

**1** *Work with a partner and complete the questionnaire above.*

**2** *What is an "American" breakfast?*

➡ **Watch The Websters.**

## AFTER YOU WATCH

*This is a picture of the Websters. True or false?*
*Check the boxes.*

|   | true | false |
|---|------|-------|
| 1 Chelsea always gets up first. | ☐ | ☐ |
| 2 Chelsea is Mikey's sister. | ☐ | ☐ |
| 3 Chelsea's dad works in the college library. | ☐ | ☐ |
| 4 Mrs. Webster likes strawberry yogurt. | ☐ | ☐ |
| 5 Mr. Webster's first name is Chris. | ☐ | ☐ |
| 6 Mrs. Webster's first name is Mary. | ☐ | ☐ |
| 7 Mr. Carter lives near the Websters. | ☐ | ☐ |
| 8 Eric is Chelsea's boyfriend. | ☐ | ☐ |

## SECTION 1  `0 0 : 0 0`

*(from the beginning to **Chelsea**: Come and meet my family.)*

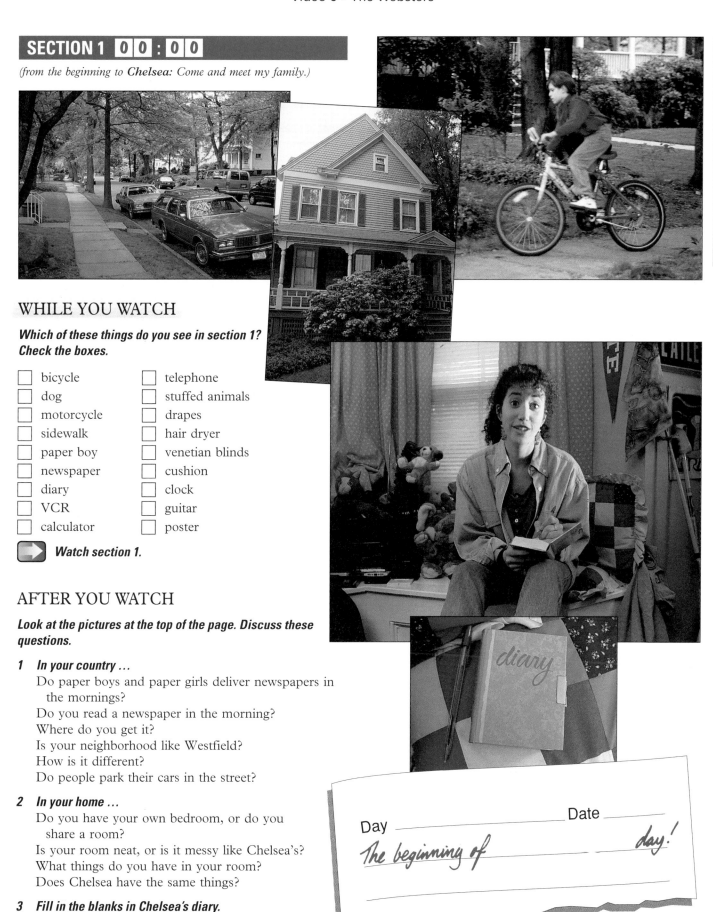

## WHILE YOU WATCH

**Which of these things do you see in section 1? Check the boxes.**

- ☐ bicycle
- ☐ dog
- ☐ motorcycle
- ☐ sidewalk
- ☐ paper boy
- ☐ newspaper
- ☐ diary
- ☐ VCR
- ☐ calculator

- ☐ telephone
- ☐ stuffed animals
- ☐ drapes
- ☐ hair dryer
- ☐ venetian blinds
- ☐ cushion
- ☐ clock
- ☐ guitar
- ☐ poster

➡️ **Watch section 1.**

## AFTER YOU WATCH

**Look at the pictures at the top of the page. Discuss these questions.**

**1  In your country …**
Do paper boys and paper girls deliver newspapers in the mornings?
Do you read a newspaper in the morning?
Where do you get it?
Is your neighborhood like Westfield?
How is it different?
Do people park their cars in the street?

**2  In your home …**
Do you have your own bedroom, or do you share a room?
Is your room neat, or is it messy like Chelsea's?
What things do you have in your room?
Does Chelsea have the same things?

**3  Fill in the blanks in Chelsea's diary.**

Day _____  Date _____
*The beginning of _____ day!*

## SECTION 2 `01`:`01`

*(to Chelsea: … My dad never listens to me.)*

## BEFORE YOU WATCH

**Who says it? Write M for Mikey, C for Chelsea, W for Mr. Webster.**

- [ ] Don't you have one?
- [ ] Can I borrow yours?
- [ ] No way.
- [ ] But I can't do my math.
- [ ] Tough.
- [ ] Is that your homework, Michael?
- [ ] I don't believe this!

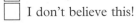 **Watch section 2.**

## AFTER YOU WATCH

**Fill in the blanks in Chelsea's sentences.**

1 Mikey _____ does his homework at breakfast.
2 He _____ borrows my stuff.
3 He _____ gives it back.
4 My dad _____ listens to me.

## SECTION 3 `01`:`54`

*(to Chelsea: … How often do you fight with your brother?)*

## WHILE YOU WATCH

**What happens in section 3? Number these sentences in the correct order from 1 to 7.**

- [ ] Chelsea takes out a spoon.
- [ ] Chelsea takes out some juice.
- [ ] Mrs. Webster opens the cabinet.
- [ ] Chelsea opens the refigerator.
- [ ] Mrs. Webster opens the refrigerator.
- [ ] Mrs. Webster takes out a mug.
- [ ] Chelsea opens the drawer.

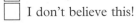 **Watch section 3.**

## AFTER YOU WATCH

**1 Choose the correct frequency adverb. Check the column.**

| | always | usually | sometimes | hardly ever | never |
|---|---|---|---|---|---|
| 1 Chelsea has orange juice for breakfast. | | | | | |
| 2 Chelsea has yogurt for breakfast. | | | | | |
| 3 Chelsea has toast for breakfast. | | | | | |
| 4 On weekends they have a hot breakfast. | | | | | |
| 5 Mrs. Webster eats breakfast. | | | | | |
| 6 The Websters don't speak at breakfast. | | | | | |

**2 Then make complete sentences, e.g.:**

Chelsea usually has orange juice for breakfast.

**3 Look back at the chart. Make sentences about yourself.**

## SECTION 4 `0 2 : 5 4`
*(to the end)*

### BEFORE YOU WATCH

*Match these sentences to the pictures. Write the number of the sentence in the box on the picture.*

1 Where's my stuff?
2 'Bye, Chelsea. Have a good day.
3 Well, that's all, folks. Have a nice day.
4 Is that the time?
5 You know what I mean?
6 Are you going to the game tonight?
7 How's it going, buddy?
8 Eric likes me …

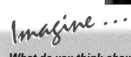

 **Watch section 4.**

### AFTER YOU WATCH

**1** *Underline the mistakes in this text, then correct them.*
Mr. Carter's their neighbor. He lives in the next town. Mr. Carter and Mr. Webster live downtown, so they carpool – they share their money. Sometimes Mr. Webster takes the subway, and sometimes Mr. Carter takes the bus. This afternoon, it's Mr. Webster's turn.

**2** *Ask and answer these questions.*
Does Eric like Chelsea?
Does Eric like Mr. and Mrs. Webster?
Do they like Eric?
Does Chelsea like Eric?
Describe him.
Describe his car.

 **Watch the whole story again.**

*Imagine …*

**1** *What do you think about Mikey's day? Compare your ideas with a partner's. There are no "correct" answers.*

What time does he usually get up?
What does he usually have for breakfast?
How does he go to school?
What's his favorite school lesson?
What does he do after school? (Make sentences with *always / often / sometimes / never*.)
How often does he fight with his sister?
What time does he usually go to bed?

**2** *Then choose ONE character from the video. Use your imagination and describe their daily routine.*

# Vocabulary

## A one-family house

**Read this description of the Webster's house. Put the bold words in the correct places on the picture.**

It's an older wood-frame house, built more than seventy years ago. It has three floors and a **basement**, where there is a furnace. The top floor is the **attic**. The house has **clapboard walls**, and wooden shingles on the **gable**. It also has a shingle **roof**. The upstairs **windows** have **shutters**. There's a **porch** around the ground floor.

## In the kitchen

**Look at the picture of the kitchen. You can find some of the words in the box below.**

Name something green.
Name something yellow.
Name something gray.
Name something you can read.
Name three things made of wood.
Name three things that make food hot.
Name the two places where you can put dirty dishes.
Name something you do not have in your kitchen.

| Vocabulary | |
|---|---|
| cabinets | microwave oven |
| can opener | outlet |
| counter | plants |
| dishwasher | plug |
| dishwashing liquid | sink |
| drawer | stove |
| faucet | toaster |

## Chelsea's bedroom

**1 Find these things in the pictures. Write "1" for picture 1, "2" for picture 2, or "1 & 2" for both pictures.**

| | | | | | |
|---|---|---|---|---|---|
| ☐ nail polish | ☐ cushions | ☐ compact |
| ☐ posters | ☐ bureau | ☐ photograph |
| ☐ pennants | ☐ ski boots | ☐ diary |
| ☐ jeans | ☐ hairbrush | ☐ lipstick |
| ☐ mirror | ☐ cartoons | ☐ wastebasket |
| ☐ skis | ☐ ski poles | ☐ picture frame |
| ☐ baseball hat | ☐ drapes | ☐ venetian blind |

**2 Look at the words again. Delete (~~delete~~) any words that you are never going to use!**

**3 Make six sentences about the pictures, using words that you want to remember. You can use the words below:**

| | |
|---|---|
| … in the corner. | … on the wall. |
| … in the drawer. | … on the bureau. |
| … by … | … next to … |
| … in front of … | … behind … |

54

# TELL THE STORY

1 **Work with a partner. Number the pictures in the correct order from 1 to 14.**

2 **Then tell the story. Make sentences about each picture.**

# Exercises

## Exercise 1

*Look at the chart. Look at the ideas below.*
*For each person, write one thing on each line.*
*The answers are your opinion.*

**place of work**
  office   library   school   bank
**sport / pastime**
  tennis   golf   computer games
  reading   swimming   chess
**magazine**
  National Geographic   Car & Driver
  Computer World   Sports News
**favorite food**
  pizza   steak   Japanese food   fries
**favorite drink**
  cola   coffee   herb tea   milk shake
**favorite music**
  opera   heavy metal   modern jazz   new age
**favorite TV program**
  Star Trek   World Series Baseball   old movies
  nature programs   MTV   The Simpsons

|  | Mrs. Webster | Eric | Mr. Carter |
|---|---|---|---|
| place of work |  |  |  |
| sport / pastime |  |  |  |
| magazine |  |  |  |
| favorite food |  |  |  |
| favorite drink |  |  |  |
| favorite music |  |  |  |
| favorite TV program |  |  |  |

## Exercise 2

*Use your chart. Make sentences, e.g.:*

Eric goes to school every day.
Mr. Carter works in an office / a bank.
Mrs. Webster works in a library.

*Try to use some of the verbs in the box.*

```
work   go   play   read   watch   listen to   like
```

## Exercise 3

*Interview your partner. Make seven sentences about your partner.*

## Exercise 4

*Word order. Make sentences, e.g.:*

Webster / hardly ever / breakfast. / Mrs./ has
Mrs. Webster hardly ever has breakfast.

1   up / gets / Mr. / at / six-thirty. / usually / Webster
2   calculator / school. / Mikey / leaves / at / often / his
3   toast / breakfast. / for / eats / Chelsea / sometimes
4   car. / Eric / his / cleans / never
5   cleans / room. / her / Chelsea / hardly ever

## Exercise 5

*headword*   *pronunciation*

**carpool** \kä'pōol\ Also car pool, car-pool. *n.* an arrangement by a group of automobile owners or drivers, in which they share a car for regular travel. They take turns driving their cars with the other members of the group as passengers. Also the group of people making the arrangement. *v.* [I] to form or join a carpool, to share a car for regular traveling.

*definition or meaning*

*grammar note (noun, verb etc)*

*Read the dictionary definition of* carpool.

In America many people carpool. In some cities there are lanes on the expressways for "carpool only" at busy times of the day.

*Answer the questions:*
Do you carpool?
Is it a good idea? Why?
Do you like sharing a ride with people?
What are the advantages and disadvantages?

# Reference

## Present simple tense: (e.g.: *like* )

AFFIRMATIVE

| I<br>You<br>We<br>They | like | coffee.<br>tennis.<br>cats.<br>him. |
|---|---|---|
| She<br>He<br>It | likes | her.<br>them. |

NEGATIVE

| I<br>You<br>We<br>They | don't<br>do not | like | coffee.<br>tennis.<br>cats.<br>him. |
|---|---|---|---|
| She<br>He<br>It | doesn't<br>does not | | her.<br>them. |

QUESTIONS AND SHORT ANSWERS

| Do | I<br>you<br>we<br>they | like | coffee?<br>tennis?<br>cats?<br>him?<br>her?<br>them? | Yes, I do. / No, I don't.<br>Yes, you do. / No, you don't.<br>Yes, we do. / No, we don't.<br>Yes, they do. / No, they don't. |
|---|---|---|---|---|
| Does | he<br>she<br>(it) | | | Yes, he does. / No, he doesn't.<br>Yes, she does. / No, she doesn't.<br>Yes, it does. / No, it doesn't. |

## Present simple tense with everyday habits

| I<br>You<br>We<br>They | work<br>don't work | every day.<br>from nine to five.<br>eight hours a day.<br>on Sundays.<br>downtown.<br>in an office.<br>for General Motors. |
|---|---|---|
| She<br>He<br>It | works<br>doesn't work | |

## Dates

May 23 1995 (*Say* "May twenty-third 1995.")
July 4 1997 (*Say* "July fourth 1997.")

*In the U.S.A. and Canada, the abbreviations for these dates are:*
  May 23 – 5/23/95 (month/day/year)
  July 4 – 7/4/97

*In most countries, including Britain, the abbreviations are 23/5/95 and 4/7/97.*

*This order (day/month/year) is also used on U.S. immigration forms and other "international" documents.*

## Frequency adverbs

| I<br>You<br>We<br>They | always<br>usually<br>often<br>sometimes | have<br>eat | lunch at 12.<br>breakfast in bed.<br>dinner at home.<br>toast with breakfast. |
|---|---|---|---|
| She<br>He<br>It | hardly ever<br>never | has<br>eats | |

WITH THE VERB *BE*

| I | 'm | always | late. |
|---|---|---|---|
| He<br>She<br>It | 's<br>is | usually<br>often<br>sometimes<br>hardly ever | busy.<br>on time.<br>early.<br>here. |
| You<br>We<br>They | 're<br>are | never | |

## Questions about frequency

| What time<br>When | do you | usually | get up?<br>have breakfast? |
|---|---|---|---|
| | does he | | |

| How often | do you | do that?<br>drive to school? |
|---|---|---|
| | does she | |

| Do you | ever | do that?<br>drive to school? |
|---|---|---|
| Does he | | |

## Expressions

Come on down!
Come and meet (my family).
No way.
Tough.
I don't believe this!
(This is) the last one.
It's (his) turn.
How are you doing?
How's it going?
Have a (good / nice) day.
See you (later) / (at seven).
You know what I mean?
I guess …
That's all, (folks).

*Video*

**SEVEN 7 SEVEN**

# Good morning, Greenstown

## BEFORE YOU WATCH

*Read these facts about radio in the U.S.A.*

☞ In 1922 one home in 500 had a radio.
In 1926 one home in 20 had a radio.
By 1930 nearly every home had one.

☞ In 1992 there were 520,000,000 radios in the U.S.A.

☞ In 1921 there were eight radio stations.
By 1922 there were 564.
Today there are nearly 10,000.
(4,619 AM stations, 3,324 FM stations, 1,106
educational FM stations)

☞ In 1928 Motorola invented the car radio.

☞ How many radios are there in different countries?
Italy – 1 to 3.9 people
Brazil – 1 to 2.5 people
Japan – 1 to 1.3
Britain – 1 to 1
Australia – 1 to 0.9
U.S.A. – 1 to 0.5. (Each person in the U.S.A. has two radios!)

☞ You hear a lot of abbreviations on radio!
Here are some common ones:
DJ – disc jockey
A.O.R. – album-oriented radio
R & B – rhythm and blues

☞ In some areas you can pick up 40 or more
local radio stations.

WATCHING THE VIDEO

## SECTION 1 `0 0 : 0 0`

*(from the beginning to Marcie: ... my breakfast.)*

### BEFORE YOU WATCH

**Which of these things does a DJ do? Check the boxes.**

- [ ] plays music
- [ ] talks during the music
- [ ] repeats his or her name frequently
- [ ] repeats the station name frequently
- [ ] gives weather reports
- [ ] tells you the time
- [ ] reads news bulletins
- [ ] presents a quiz
- [ ] speaks to phone callers
- [ ] tells jokes
- [ ] tells you the name of the singer or band
- [ ] tells you the position of a record in the Top 40
- [ ] plays commercials
- [ ] interviews famous people

### WHILE YOU WATCH

**Underline the things the DJ does in section 1.**

 **Watch section 1.**

### AFTER YOU WATCH

**1  Fill in the blanks.**

## WHAT-FM GREENSTOWN
### ☎ 5-3-5 W-H-A-T

**Day:** Thursday      **Date:** May 25

**Program title:**

**Program times:**

**DJ:** Greg Tyler

**Producer:** Marcie Simpson

**Time now:**

**Temperature:**      °Fahrenheit

**Weather:**

---

**2  Answer the questions.**
Are there any quiz questions in front of Greg?
Are they today's questions?
Which questions are they?
Were today's questions there a moment ago?
Are they in the trash?
What is in the trash?
Whose breakfast was it?

## SECTION 2 `0 1 : 2 0`

*(to Greg: ... Too bad!)*

### BEFORE YOU WATCH

**Look back at section 1 BEFORE YOU WATCH. What is Greg going to do in section 2? Choose two more things from the list.**

 **Watch section 2.**

### AFTER YOU WATCH

**1  Fill in the blanks.**

**Greg:** That was Tanisha's new single. It's a big hit. She was number nine _____ week. She's number five _____ week. Is she going to be number one _____ week?

**2  Imagine you're a DJ. Change the underlined words. Replace them with your own words.**

**Greg:** You're listening to <u>Greg Tyler</u>. It's <u>ten thirty-five</u>, and it's time for the <u>Greg Tyler Rock Quiz</u>, your chance to win <u>this week's top ten CDs</u>. Pick up the phone and call <u>5-3-5 WHAT</u> now ...

*Practice being a DJ. Greg's speech was 16 seconds long. How fast can you read YOUR speech? Ask someone to time you.*

**3  Answer the questions.**
What was Greg's question?
What was Tom's answer?
Was it correct?
Do you know the correct answer?

**WATCHING THE VIDEO**

## SECTION 3  `0 2` : `3 0`

*(to **Greg**: … Stay with us.)*

## BEFORE YOU WATCH (1)

***Can you write two more questions for Greg's quiz?
(You can change it from a Rock quiz to a Music quiz or a
General Knowledge quiz if you like.)***

 **Watch section 3.**

## BEFORE YOU WATCH (2)

***Work with a partner. Number these pictures in the correct
sequence from 1 to 5.***
***Ask questions, e.g.:***
Was this one first or was it second?
Which one was next? etc.

 **Watch section 3 again.**

## AFTER YOU WATCH

***1 What happened? Are these sentences true or false?
Check the boxes. Correct the false sentences.***

<table>
<tr><td></td><td></td><td>true</td><td>false</td></tr>
<tr><td>1</td><td>Crystal didn't know the answers.</td><td>☐</td><td>☐</td></tr>
<tr><td>2</td><td>Elvis Presley's first number-one record<br>was "You're a Heartbreaker."</td><td>☐</td><td>☐</td></tr>
<tr><td>3</td><td>Marcie dropped "The Beatles" card.</td><td>☐</td><td>☐</td></tr>
<tr><td>4</td><td>Greg knew the answer to The Beatles<br>question.</td><td>☐</td><td>☐</td></tr>
<tr><td>5</td><td>Crystal screamed when she got the<br>correct answers.</td><td>☐</td><td>☐</td></tr>
<tr><td>6</td><td>Greg went to the Titanium concert last<br>week.</td><td>☐</td><td>☐</td></tr>
<tr><td>7</td><td>Buddy Holly died in a plane crash.</td><td>☐</td><td>☐</td></tr>
<tr><td>8</td><td>Crystal won the prize.</td><td>☐</td><td>☐</td></tr>
<tr><td>9</td><td>The quiz finished at ten forty-three.</td><td>☐</td><td>☐</td></tr>
</table>

***2 Write the past tenses of these verbs:***

do          _____
know        _____
die         _____
is          _____
scream      _____
win         _____
drop        _____
go          _____
finish      _____

## SECTION 4 ⏱ 04:26

*(to the end)*

### BEFORE YOU WATCH (1)

***Greg is going to interview Paloma Lee, a movie star.
What is he going to ask her about? Guess.***

 ***Watch section 4.***

### BEFORE YOU WATCH (2)

***Match Greg's sentences with Paloma's responses.***

1  Tell us about the movie, Paloma.
2  Your costar?
3  Did he go to the premiere with you last night?
4  Did Donny come with you to Greenstown?
5  Donny is a … dolphin?
6  And are you going to make another movie with Donny?

A  Yeah, Donny.
B  Donny is a wild animal, Greg.
C  No …
D  Thank you, Greg.
E  Excuse me?
F  That's right, Greg.

 ***Watch section 4 again.***

## AFTER YOU WATCH

1  ***Greg made some bad mistakes during the interview. He
    said the wrong things:***

- ☐ It's a fantastic movie, and I really enjoyed it.
- ☐ Did he go to the premiere with you last night?
- ☐ Did Donny come with you to Greenstown?
- ☐ And are you going to make another movie with Donny?
- ☐ And the next record's for you, Donny … wherever you are.

### *Why were they wrong?*

- Two were *mistakes* (because he didn't know anything about the movie). Write M next to these sentences.
- In one, Greg didn't think about the needs of wild animals (animal rights). He was *thoughtless*. Write T next to this one.
- One was *stupid* or *dumb*. Write S next to this one.
- One was a *lie*. He wasn't telling the truth. Write L next to the lie.

2  ***Ask and answer these questions:***

When did Paloma fly into Greenstown?
Why did she come to Greenstown?
Where was the premiere?
Where did Paloma make the movie?
Did she like her costar?
What was his name?
What happened to Donny after the movie?

 ***Watch the whole story again.***

## *Imagine …*

CLASS FM
***Imagine that you're a DJ for your class radio station.
You are going to do these three things:***

- introduce yourself and the station, give the time and weather today;
- introduce a favorite record;
- interview someone from your class about their last vacation, or about last weekend.

***Time your "program." You can record it on audio or video
tape if you like.***

WATCHING THE VIDEO

# Vocabulary

## Audio equipment

*How many of the words below can you find in the picture of the studio? Are any of them the same (or nearly the same) in your language?*

| | |
|---|---|
| microphone | telephone |
| headphones | reel-to-reel tape recorder |
| CDs | personal stereo |
| speaker | mixing console |
| cassettes | VCR |

## Music

*In the U.S.A. you can find a radio station for almost any kind of music. Here are some types of radio station. Compare American radio with radio in your country.*

| | |
|---|---|
| Top 40 | Usually AM radio. Plays the Top-40 singles. |
| A.O.R. | "Album-oriented radio." Always FM stereo. Plays album tracks. |
| Golden oldies | Plays old hits. Often there's a "60s" program or a "70s" program. |
| Classic rock | Plays old album tracks. |
| Country | Usually plays "new country" music (but also some older "country and western"). |
| College radio | Often transmitted from college radio stations. Plays new music for a student audience. |
| R & B | Plays African American music. In big cities there may be separate stations for rhythm and blues, soul / disco, and rap. |

You can also find jazz stations, news-only stations, Spanish language stations (with Latin American music), and classical music stations.

## Reading: past tenses

*Underline all the past tense verbs in this text.*

### Buddy Holly: The day the music died

Buddy Holly was born in Lubbock, Texas, in 1937. He had several hit records between 1957 and 1959 with his band, The Crickets. Some of his hits were "That'll Be the Day," "Peggy Sue," "Oh Boy!," "Listen to Me," and "Rave On!" He was one of the first rock "singer-songwriters" – he wrote his own material. (The Beatles were great fans of Buddy Holly.) In August 1958, Buddy married Maria Elena Santiago. They moved to New York, and The Crickets returned to Texas. Buddy needed money. He joined a 24-date tour of the Midwest ("The Winter Dance Party") with other rock stars — Ritchie Valens, The Big Bopper, and Dion. The weather was terrible, with below-zero temperatures. The musicians traveled by bus, often for ten or twelve hours a day. After a concert at Clear Lake, Iowa, Holly decided to fly to Fargo, North Dakota, for the next concert. He hired a small plane. Valens and The Big Bopper came with him. Valens won his seat on the plane after he tossed a coin with Holly's guitarist. The plane crashed in bad weather a few minutes after takeoff, in a field near Mason City, Iowa. The three singers and the pilot all died. That was February 3, 1959. Buddy had more hits after his death. The first one was "It Doesn't Matter Anymore." ∎

# TELL THE STORY

**What happened in Good morning, Greenstown? Tell the story using the past tense. You can use some of the verbs in the box.**

| |
|---|
| asked |
| answered |
| called |
| interviewed |
| introduced |
| gave |
| found |
| saw |
| showed |
| wrote |
| heard |
| drank |
| spoke |
| said |

**3**

```
WHAT-FM GREENSTOWN

Good Morning Show
with Greg Tyler

Weather report: Greenstown

Thursday May 25  morning
73°F (23°C)
sunny skies all day

Friday May 26 all day
54°F (12°C) rain,
thunderstorms, tornados?
```

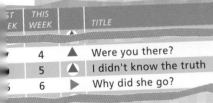

| ST EK | THIS WEEK | | TITLE | ARTIST | LABEL |
|---|---|---|---|---|---|
| | 4 | ▲ | Were you there? | **Maria King** | River |
| | 5 | ▲ | I didn't know the truth | Tanisha | Bronco |
| | 6 | ▶ | Why did she go? | **Garth Cook** | Western |

1959

SWIM FREE

# Exercises

## Exercise 1

***Ask and answer questions about the chart, e.g.:***

Which band / Who was number five last week?
Where were The Funsters last week?
Where are they this week?
Where is Princess this week?
Where was she last week?

## Exercise 2

***These are the real questions for The Greg Tyler Rock Quiz.***

**WHAT-FM GREENSTOWN**
**The Greg Tyler Rock Quiz. Questions**
Thursday May 25

**1 EASY**
When did Elvis Presley die?
**A:** 1967 **B:** 1957 **C:** 1977

**2 MEDIUM**
Were Madonna's family …
**A:** Italian - American?
**B:** Greek - American?
**C:** Native American?

**3 DIFFICULT**
Who wrote "Blowing in the Wind"?
**A:** Joan Baez
**B:** Peter, Paul & Mary
**C:** Bob Dylan

**(4 extra question – VERY DIFFICULT – for callers you don't like )**
What type of guitar did Paul McCartney play on early Beatles records?
**A:** Fender Bass
**B:** Hofner Violin Bass
**C:** Yamaha Bass

**WHAT-FM GREENSTOWN**
**The Greg Tyler Rock Quiz. Questions**
Wednesday May 24

**1 EASY**
When was Michael Jackson born?
**A:** 1968 **B:** 1958 **C:** 1978

**2 MEDIUM**
Which group sang "I Want to Hold Your Hand"?
**A:** The Monkees
**B:** The Jackson 5
**C:** The Beatles

**3 DIFFICULT**
Where did Elvis Presley live?
**A:** Memphis, Tennessee
**B:** Las Vegas, Nevada
**C:** Hollywood, California

**(4 extra question – VERY DIFFICULT – for callers you don't like )**
What was the catalog number of The Beatles' album "Yesterday and Today"?
**A:** FZ-1498 **B:** ST-2553 **C:** BE-6074

***Greg asks THREE questions. He can choose which three. He can help the caller if he wants, e.g.:***

**Greg:** Your first question. When did Buddy Holly die?
**Caller:** Uh … uh … Buddy Holly?
**Greg:** That's right. Did he die in 1959? Did he die in 1969? Or did he die in 1979?
**Caller:** He died in 1969 (OR 1959).
**Greg:** Oh, no! He didn't! Sorry. (OR Yes, that's correct.)

***Try the quiz with a partner. Student A uses Thursday's questions, student B uses Wednesday's questions. The answers are on page 80.***

**WHAT-FM GREENSTOWN**
**Tel: 5-3-5 W-H-A-T**
**Top 20 countdown** Week beginning: Sunday May 21

| LAST WEEK | THIS WEEK | | TITLE | ARTIST | LABEL |
|---|---|---|---|---|---|
| 2 | 1 | ▲ | Never say always | Streetwise inc. | Batter |
| 5 | 2 | ▲ | Gave a letter to my mailman | Alvis P. | Gold |
| 1 | 3 | ▼ | Electric nightmare | The Plus | A.R.C. |
| 7 | 4 | ▲ | Were you there? | Maria King | River |
| 9 | 5 | ▲ | I didn't know the truth | Tanisha | Bronco |
| 6 | 6 | ▶ | Why did she go? | Garth Cook | Western |
| 12 | 7 | ▲ | Peggy Sue got married | Buddy Holly | Revive! |
| 39 | 8 | ▲ | Tried, lied, died | New Gang | R.I.P. |
| 3 | 9 | ▼ | When you were mine | Princess | Purple |
| 4 | 10 | ▼ | It went that way! | The Funsters | Novelty |
| 11 | 11 | ▶ | I sang an old song, baby | Bud Dolan | Tarantula |
| 9 | 12 | | Sooner or later | Iron Lady | Excalibur |

# Reference

## was / were

AFFIRMATIVE AND NEGATIVE

| I | was | here. |
| He | wasn't | there. |
| She | was not | late. |
| It | | at home. |
| We | were | correct. |
| You | weren't | wrong. |
| They | were not | |

QUESTIONS AND SHORT ANSWERS

| Was | I | here? |
| | he | there? |
| | she | late? |
| | it | at home? |
| Were | we | correct? |
| | you | wrong? |
| | they | |

| Yes, I was. / No, I wasn't. |
| Yes, he was. / No, he wasn't. |
| Yes, she was. / No, she wasn't. |
| Yes, it was. / No, it wasn't. |
| Yes, we were. / No, we weren't. |
| Yes, you were. / No, you weren't. |
| Yes, they were. / No, they weren't. |

## Past simple tense

AFFIRMATIVE

| I | went | to school | yesterday. |
| You | came | | last week. |
| She | drove | | last month. |
| He | walked | | last year. |
| It | traveled | | last Tuesday. |
| We | | | on Monday. |
| They | | | at 8 o'clock. |

NEGATIVE

| I | didn't | go | to school | yesterday. |
| You | did not | come | | last week. |
| She | | drive | | last month. |
| He | | walk | | last year. |
| It | | travel | | last Tuesday. |
| We | | | | on Monday. |
| They | | | | at 8 o'clock. |

QUESTIONS AND SHORT ANSWERS

| Did | I | go | to school | yesterday? |
| Didn't | you | come | | last week? |
| | he | drive | | last month? |
| | she | walk | | last year? |
| | it | travel | | last Tuesday? |
| | we | | | on Monday? |
| | they | | | at 8 o'clock? |

| Yes, I did. / No, I didn't. |
| Yes, you did. / No, you didn't. |
| Yes, he did. / No, he didn't. |
| Yes, she did. / No, she didn't. |
| Yes, it did. / No, it didn't. |
| Yes, we did. / No, we didn't. |
| Yes, they did. / No, they didn't. |

What did you do?
Where did you go?
Who did you see?

## Possessive pronouns

The prize is yours!

| mine |
| yours |
| his |
| hers |
| ours |
| theirs |

## Regular and irregular verbs

| regular | | irregular | |
| --- | --- | --- | --- |
| **present** | **past** | **present** | **past** |
| listen | listened | do | did |
| call | called | have | had |
| enjoy | enjoyed | go | went |
| stay | stayed | come | came |
| play | played | become | became |
| die | died | see | saw |
| release | released | know | knew |
| die | died | fly | flew |
| believe | believed | tell | told |
| | | make | made |
| | | win | won |
| | | take | took |

## Expressions

Are you having a good time?
Can you believe that?
Relax …
What do I do?
It's time for …
(It's) your chance to win …
on the line
Too bad.
Take it easy.
(not) my kind of music
Have a seat.
Welcome to …
 … a lot of fun
Excuse me?
wherever you are

# Video

## 8

EIGHT • EIGHT

# The Artist

## BEFORE YOU WATCH

**What do you know about modern art? Can you answer any of these questions? Answer on your own, and check with the class.**

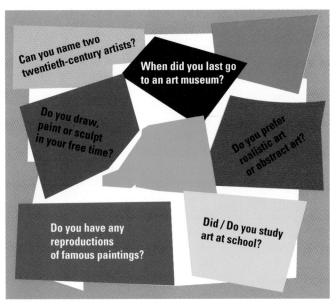

Can you name two twentieth-century artists?

When did you last go to an art museum?

Do you draw, paint or sculpt in your free time?

Do you prefer realistic art or abstract art?

Do you have any reproductions of famous paintings?

Did / Do you study art at school?

 **Watch The Artist.**

## AFTER YOU WATCH

**Identify the people in the pictures. Match the sentences.**

The one on the top left is ...            ... the art critic.
The one on the bottom left is ...         ... the male visitor.
The one in the top center is ...          ... the female visitor.
The one in the bottom center is ...       ... the security guard.
The one on the top right is ...           ... the gallery owner.
The one on the bottom right is ...        ... the artist.

## SECTION 1  0 0 : 0 0

*(from the beginning to when the artist leaves the gallery)*

## BEFORE YOU WATCH

**Who says it? Write A for the artist, G for the gallery owner.**

- [ ] I want to show you my work.
- [ ] And you want to exhibit it here?
- [ ] Let me see it, then.
- [ ] I'm trying to sell my pictures.
- [ ] May I suggest something?
- [ ] Maybe I'll see you in a year or two, mm?
- [ ] Thank you for your time.

 **Watch section 1.**

## AFTER YOU WATCH

**1  Answer the questions.**

Does her gallery exhibit new artists?

Is she really interested in the painting?

Does she really want to see the artist again?

Does she think she'll see the artist again?

**2  Choose words to describe the gallery owner (you can use a dictionary):**

- [ ] polite   [ ] honest   [ ] kind   [ ] friendly
- [ ] condescending   [ ] superior

When did she come to New York?

Why did she come to New York?

Where was she at art school?

Does she agree with the gallery owner's suggestions?

Will she come back in a year or two?

**3  Choose words to describe the artist's feelings:**

- [ ] disappointed   [ ] angry   [ ] unhappy
- [ ] hurt   [ ] proud of her work

**4  Match the sentence to the function.**

| sentence | function |
|---|---|
| Can I help you? | *suggestion* |
| Let me see it then. | *explanation* |
| But I'm sorry. We can't exhibit it here. | *request* |
| You see, we only exhibit well-known artists. | *apology* |
| Why don't you spend some time in the art museums here in New York? | *offer* |

WATCHING THE VIDEO

## SECTION 2 `01:55`

*(to **Man**: … look at the Andy Warhols.)*

## BEFORE YOU WATCH

**Look at the picture.**
Who painted it?
When did he paint it?
How big is it?
When was he born?
When did he die?

**Choose words to describe the painting:**

- [ ] brilliant
- [ ] a work of genius
- [ ] interesting
- [ ] abstract
- [ ] realistic
- [ ] boring
- [ ] complete trash
- [ ] beautiful
- [ ] depressing

WALTER STROHEIM
(1898 - 1973)
*Mid-life Crisis, 1947*
Oil on canvas.
30 inches x 20 inches
(76 x 51 cm)

 **Watch section 2.**

## AFTER YOU WATCH

**<u>Underline</u> the mistakes in this transcript, then correct them.**

**Man:** It's a work of happiness.
A friend of mine won a Stroheim.
It cost a few hundred dollars,
and it was only a Disney cartoon.
The museum made ten billion, I
believe. That was twenty days
ago. Of course, Stroheim lived
in Tunis for many years, and he
painted in different colors. He
bought this one in 1947.

## SECTION 3 `03:24`

*(to when the art critic arrives)*

## BEFORE YOU WATCH

**Number these sentences in the correct order from 1 to 8.**

- [ ] The guard left the room.
- [ ] She took out her painting.
- [ ] She sat down on the chair.
- [ ] She went over to the Stroheim.
- [ ] She stuck her painting on top of the Stroheim.
- [ ] She opened her coat.
- [ ] The guard spoke to her.
- [ ] She looked around.

 **Watch section 3.**

## AFTER YOU WATCH

**Answer these questions.**
Does the guard have a sister?
How old is she?
Is she a famous artist?
Can she paint?
Are her paintings worth ten million dollars?
What does the guard think of the Stroheim?
Do you agree with him?

## SECTION 4  0 5 : 1 3

*(to the end)*

### BEFORE YOU WATCH

**Write the numbers of the pictures next to the correct sentences below.**

- [ ] This is new, isn't it?
- [ ] I love this one!
- [ ] Funny. It looks familiar.
- [ ] My kid sister paints like that, and she's only three years old.
- [ ] I'm an art critic.
- [ ] Yes!

 **Watch section 4.**

### AFTER YOU WATCH

**Who said it? Write G for the gallery owner, C for the art critic, A for the artist.**

- [ ] He painted in so many different styles.
- [ ] I want to see the Picassos.
- [ ] I'll see you later.
- [ ] I'll meet you by the entrance.
- [ ] Yes, I agree with you.
- [ ] Nice meeting you.

 **Watch the whole story again.**

*Imagine . . .*

**What's going to happen next?**

Will the artist tell anyone?
Will she tell her friends? / the art critic? / the gallery owner? / the security guard? / a newspaper?
Will she get her painting back?
Will that be easy or difficult?
How can she get it?
How will the art critic feel?
How will the gallery owner feel?

# Vocabulary

## Shapes and colors (1)

*Do you have a computer? Do you have a graphics program? This is a computer screen from a "paint" program. You can see the tool menu on the left. What are the tools? Put the words in the boxes.*

oval            circle
polygon         rectangle
line            eraser
paintbrush      aerosol
fill (with color)   text
color wheel (choose colors)
freehand pencil (draw what you like)

| TOOLS | |
|---|---|
| *color wheel* | |
| | |
| | |
| | |
| | |

**File  Edit  Options  Windows  Draw  Paint  Font  Size  Style**

**Peter's Painting**

Tools

## Shapes and colors (2): Location

**Make sentences about the computer painting, e.g.:**

The light-blue triangle is on the top left / in the top left corner.

**Use these words:**

colors:
pink    orange
brown   purple
red     dark blue
gray

shapes:
square  star
triangle oval
rectangle circle
polygon  line

## Prices and value

Fill in the blanks in the text, using words from the box.

cost   worth   paid   money   sold   bought

Stroheim _____ the painting to a restaurant owner in 1947 for a few French francs, and _____ a hamburger with the _____ . The museum _____ ten million dollars for it in 1975. It's _____ about fifteen million dollars now. A private collector bought a small Stroheim pencil cartoon last year. It _____ two hundred thousand dollars.

## Describing people

**condescend (to somebody)** \ˈkändəˌsend\ *verb* [I] to behave towards somebody in a way that shows you think you are better or more important than they are. **condescending** *adj.* *a condescending smile.*

**know-it-all** \ˈnō itˌôl\ *noun.* someone who thinks they know everything.

**pretentious** \prēˈtenchəs\ *adj.* trying to appear more serious or important than you really are: *a pretentious modern movie* ☞ the opposite is **unpretentious**.

**proud** \ˈpraud\ *adj.* **1 proud (of somebody/something); proud (to do something)** feeling pleased and satisfied about something that you own or did: *They are very proud of their new apartment; a proud mother of twins* **2** not wanting help from other people: *He was too proud to ask for help.* **3** feeling that you are better than other people: *Now that she's Chief Executive Officer, she'll be too proud to talk to us.*

**Look at the dictionary definitions and answer these questions.**

1 Which meaning of *proud* describes the artist, 1, 2 or 3?
2 Is *know-it-all* an adjective, a verb, or a noun?
3 Who is a know-it-all in The Artist?
4 How many of the people in the video are pretentious? Is the guard pretentious?
5 Who condescends to the artist?
6 *Condescend* is a verb. What's the adjective from condescend?

# TELL THE STORY

*What happened? Tell the story of The Artist. Try to make a sentence about each picture, and also say what happened between the pictures.*

# Exercises

## Exercise 1

South building — second floor galleries

| Action painters<br>Pollock | American Art 1945-1960<br>Stroheim<br>Oldenberg<br>Johns | Sculptures<br>Moore<br>Giaccometti<br>Smith | Pop Art<br>Warhol<br>Lichtenstein | rest rooms |
| --- | --- | --- | --- | --- |
| Surrealists<br>Dali<br>Ernst | gift store | entrance | European artists<br>Picasso<br>Mondrian | |

**Make conversations with a partner, e.g.:**

A: I want to see the **Mondrians**. I'll see you **later**.
B: OK. I'll meet you **by the stairs**.

**Change the words in bold. Here are some ideas:**

**Artists:** See the plan above.
**Times:** later / in half an hour / in twenty minutes, etc.
**Location:** by the stairs / in the European artists gallery / by the Dalis / near the Oldenbergs, etc.

## Exercise 2

**NEW STROHEIM AT ART MUSEUM**
by our art critic —————

Brilliant! That's the only word for it. I saw the art museum's new Stroheim yesterday, and it's <u>very</u> exciting. Stroheim hardly ever worked with bright colors. Between 1946 and 1953 (the Paris years) he usually painted only in black, white, and gray, with occasional small dashes of other colors. In this 1947 painting Stroheim used red, green, <u>and</u> blue! This is very different from his other work, but of course he painted in so many different styles. The title is "Mid-life Crisis" (but Stroheim painted 23 other pictures with the same title). I guess this is "Mid-life Crisis #24"! Go see it now!

**1 Answer the questions.**

When did the art critic see the painting?
How often did Stroheim use bright colors?
Where did Stroheim live between 1946 and 1953?
What colors did he usually paint with at that time?
What's the title?
How many Stroheim paintings have this title?

**2 Tomorrow the art critic will hear the truth about the painting. <u>Underline</u> all the things he'll be sorry about writing!**

## Exercise 3

***What's the title? Can you think of titles for these pictures? There are some ideas below. Maybe you can think of some different ones!***

"The Ocean in Winter"
"Great Ideas"
"The Falling City"
"Under the Ocean"
"Expressways"
"Black Spaghetti #32"
"Earthquake"
"Worried Mind"
"Only in America"
"Me, My, Mine"
"Fish Bones"
"Chaos Theory'

## Exercise 4

**1 Follow the instructions and draw a picture.**

Draw a large rectangle. Put a circle in the center. Then put a triangle below the circle, and a small star above the circle. Draw an oval inside the circle. Now draw another triangle in the bottom right of the rectangle, and a line between the two triangles.

**2 Give instructions to your partner for a new picture.**

## A true story: a note from the writers

We wrote *The Artist* at the beginning of December, and videotaped it at the end of the following May. On May 4 we read a report in *The New York Times*. This is what happened.

On Friday April 29 a 33-year-old artist, Paul Rebhan, went into the Museum of Modern Art in New York. He put a painting in a third-floor gallery near famous paintings by Jasper Johns, Robert Motherwell and Claes Oldenberg. He stuck it to the wall with double-sided adhesive tape. He also stuck a small card on the wall, "Gift of Mr. and Mrs. Donald Trump." Museum officials didn't notice the new painting until Sunday May 1. The artist spent some time in the museum and watched visitors. One couple talked about his picture for fifteen minutes.

# Reference

## Future simple tense

AFFIRMATIVE AND NEGATIVE

| I | 'll | do it | tomorrow. |
|---|-----|-------|-----------|
| You | will | be here | next week. |
| She | won't | | next year. |
| He | will not | | next month. |
| It | | | on Saturday. |
| We | | | at 5 o'clock. |
| They | | | later. |

QUESTIONS AND SHORT ANSWERS

| Will | I | do it | tomorrow? |
|------|---|-------|-----------|
| | you | be here | next week? |
| | she | | next year? |
| | he | | next month? |
| | it | | on Saturday? |
| | we | | at 5 o'clock? |
| | they | | later? |

| |
|---|
| Yes, I will. / No, I won't. |
| Yes, you will. / No, you won't. |
| Yes, she will. / No, she won't. |
| Yes, he will. / No, he won't. |
| Yes, it will. / No, it won't. |
| Yes, we will. / No, we won't. |
| Yes, they will. / No, they won't. |

## Regular and irregular verbs

| regular | | irregular | |
|---------|------|-----------|------|
| present | past | present | past |
| show | showed | buy | bought |
| look | looked | cost | cost |
| live | lived | leave | left |
| study | studied | make | made |
| paint | painted | pay | paid |
| exhibit | exhibited | put | put |
| want | wanted | sell | sold |
| | | sit | sat |
| | | speak | spoke |
| | | spend | spent |
| | | stick | stuck |
| | | take | took |

## *Want to (do)*

| I | want | to | show | you | my | work. |
|---|------|-----|------|-----|-----|-------|
| You | 'd like | | give | him | his | painting. |
| We | | | | her | her | picture. |
| They | | | | us | our | drawing. |
| | | | | them | their | |
| | | | | me | your | |
| He | wants | | | | the | |
| She | 'd like | | | | this | |

## *Let*

Let's go there (= Let us go there. *a suggestion*)
Let me see it. (= Allow me to see it. *asking for permission*)
Let me do it. (= Allow me to do it. *an offer*)

## *... isn't it?*

That's a Stroheim, isn't it?
This is new, isn't it?

## Suggestions

Let's go there.
Why don't we go there?
May I suggest something?

## Arrangements

I'll see you later.
I'll meet you by the entrance.

## Expressions

Can I help you?
You see ...
Who knows?
Maybe ...
Thank you for your time.
You're welcome.
... a work of genius.
Oh, really?
How much is (this one) worth?
... I believe.
Of course ...
So what do you think of it?
Brilliant. / Fascinating.
No way.
Funny.
It looks (familiar).
I'll see you later.
I agree with you.
Nice meeting you.

# Transcripts

## Duane and Donna in New York

**Duane:** Wow! We're here! This is New York!
**Donna:** New York! Oh, hi. Um, I'm Donna, and he's Duane.
**Duane:** Hi. I'm Duane. And she's Donna. We're from Minnesota. This is our first day in New York City.
**Donna:** Our first day! Come on!

**Duane:** Hey, the Trump Tower.
**Donna:** Wow!

**Duane:** Wow! This is an excellent hotel.
**Doorman:** Can I help you, sir... ma'am?
**Duane:** How much is a room here?
**Doorman:** Six hundred dollars.
**Duane:** A week?
**Doorman:** A night.
**Duane & Donna:** Ouch!

**Donna:** Hotels. Very expensive... expensive... moderate... ah, budget. Fifty dollars a night. No!
**Duane:** No problem. Friends in New York. Telephone numbers... free rooms. Where's a phone booth?

**Duane:** Six... seven... two, three... eight... nine... five. Hi, Franklin?... How are you doing?... It's Duane... Duane. From Minnesota. M... I... N... E ... (*to Donna*) How do you spell it?
**Donna:** Double n. It's double n.
**Duane:** Oh ... it's M... I... double N... E... S... O... T... A... Oh, Duane! Right. D... U... A... No. D. D... U... A... N... E. Franklin? Franklin? Franklin, are you there?

**Donna:** Four one zero, two nine three three. Hi. This is Donna from Minnesota. Yeah! Is Marsha there? No?

**Duane:** Duane. D... U... A... N... E?

**Donna:** Linda! Hi! It's me. That's right! Donna. I'm in New York...

**Duane:** D... U... A... N... E? Yes, yes.

**Duane:** This is the place. There's the lake, and we're south of the lake. That's it. By the fountain. OK, look for Max.
**Donna:** Duane, uh, who is Max? Is he from college?
**Duane:** Uh... I'm not sure.
**Donna:** What do you mean?
**Duane:** I don't know. He isn't my friend. He's a friend of Michael's.
**Donna:** Oh.
**Duane & Donna:** Ouch!

**Max:** Duane?
**Duane:** Hey, Max!
**Max:** Hey, man.
**Duane:** This is Donna.
**Max:** Hey, Donna. OK, you guys, follow me.

**Duane:** Hey, Max!
**Donna:** Wait for us! Max! Max, wait!

## First Day

**Ashley:** Hi. I'm Ashley. The new help.
**Tammy:** Uh-huh. You're early.
**Ashley:** This is my first job.
**Tammy:** Uh-huh. I'm Tammy. Nice to meet you.
**Ashley:** You too. Are you the manager?
**Tammy:** Me? No, hon. I'm just a server.
**Ashley:** I'm a college student. This is a part-time job. I'm a psychology major.
**Tammy:** Oh, really? The uniforms are in the closet. This way. Here are the uniforms. Go ahead and choose one.

**Ashley:** OK. How is it?
**Tammy:** It's fabulous! It's a uniform! Come and meet the chef. His name's Brandon.
**Tammy:** Hey, Brandon!
**Brandon:** Yes?
**Tammy:** This is Ashley. She's the new help.
**Brandon:** Hi.

**Brandon:** OK. The club sandwiches are your job.

**Ashley:** The club sandwiches?

**Brandon:** We're famous for our club sandwiches. OK. Here are some slices of bread. Here's some lettuce, there's some turkey, some bacon, slices of tomato, mayonnaise and some coleslaw.

Watch me. First the bread, then one piece of turkey. Put some lettuce on the turkey, then another piece of bread, right? Next, some slices of tomato, and some bacon, then another piece of lettuce, and some mayonnaise. Finally, bread on top. OK. Now you.

**Ashley:** OK!

**Brandon:** No rings! There's a customer, Ashley.

**Ashley:** Good morning, sir. I'm Ashley and I'm your server today. Can I help you?

**Mr. Winthrop:** Special club sandwich and an orange juice, please.

**Ashley:** Coming right up.

**Tammy:** That's Harrison Winthrop.

**Ashley:** Who's Harrison Winthrop?

**Tammy:** You don't know? He's a lawyer. A real important lawyer. He's the Winthrop in Franklin, Mather, Winthrop and Franklin …

**Ashley:** There you go, sir. Enjoy your meal.

**Mr. Winthrop:** Thank you.

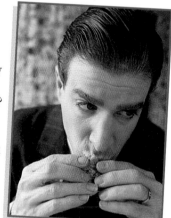

**Ashley:** My ring! Where's my ring?

**Tammy:** Is it on the counter?

**Ashley:** No!

**Tammy:** Under here? No … oh, no! The sandwich! Is it in the club sandwich?

**Brandon:** What's this?

**Ashley:** My ring!

**Brandon:** And what is this?

## Strange Encounter

**Britanny:** What's wrong?

**Scott:** I don't know. OK, turn the key. Try again.

**Britanny:** Scott …

**Scott:** What?

**Britanny:** There's someone behind you.

**Vega:** Good morning.

**Britanny:** Hello.

**Scott:** Uh, hello.

**Vega:** Pardon me. Is this the road to Rockport?

**Britanny:** Yes. Yes, it is.

**Vega:** I don't have a car.

**Britanny:** Uh, OK … come with us.

**Scott:** But … But we have a problem with the engine.

**Vega:** The engine is fine. Go ahead. Try it.

**Scott:** Please, get in.

**Britanny:** The seat belt's right there.

**Vega:** The seat belt?

**Britanny:** Fasten the belt. That's right.

**Scott:** Strange clothes!

**Vega:** Ah, yes … my clothes. I'm in a movie. I'm a movie star. They're shooting the movie in Rockport.

**Scott:** Oh, you're in a movie. I'm Scott, this is Britanny. We're on vacation.

**Vega:** How do you do? My name is Vega,

**Britanny:** Vega? That's a nice name. Where are you from?

**Vega:** My home is a long way from here. I'm in the United States for a movie.

**Britanny:** So, you aren't American.

**Vega:** No.

**Scott:** There you go. This is it. This is Rockport.

**Vega:** Thank you, Scott. Britanny?

**Britanny:** Vega! Wait! Scott, take a picture of us.

**Scott:** OK. Give me a big smile. Great!

**Britanny:** Are there any pictures left, Scott?

**Scott:** Yeah, there are two shots left.

**Britanny:** Give me the camera. That's great! Thanks, Vega.

**Vega:** You're welcome.

**Scott:** One hour processing, please.

**Clerk:** Sure. Ready at four o'clock, OK?

**Scott:** Fine.

**Britanny:** Hey, Scott. Get two sets of prints, one for Vega.

**Scott:** OK. Make that two sets of prints, please.

**Britanny:** And Scott, we don't have anymore film.

**Scott:** OK. Do you have 35-millimeter?

**Clerk:** Twenty-four or thirty-six exposure?
**Scott:** Thirty-six. Do you have Kodak Gold?
**Clerk:** Sure.
**Scott:** How much is that?
**Clerk:** Seven ninety-five.
**Scott:** Seven ninety-five.
**Clerk:** Out of twenty. That's ten ... eleven ... twelve dollars, and five cents. There you go.
**Scott:** Thanks.
**Clerk:** You're welcome.

**Britanny:** Where's Vega? Pardon me. Officer! We're looking for a friend.
**Police officer:** Uh-huh.
**Britanny:** She's in a movie here in Rockport.
**Police officer:** A movie? Here? What does she look like?
**Britanny:** She's average height. About thirty. Good looking. She's wearing a silver one-piece suit and gold boots.
**Scott:** And she has strange hair. She looks kind of weird. Like an alien.
**Police officer:** An alien. Are you kidding?
**Britanny:** She's a movie star.
**Police officer:** Look, I don't have time for this, guys. Sorry.

**Scott:** Be careful, Britanny! Don't fall in.
**Brittany:** It's beautiful here.
**Scott:** Hey, it's nearly four.

**Police officer:** Hey. Hey!

**Britanny:** OK, show me the shots of Vega.
**Scott:** That's strange! She's not here.
**Britanny:** What do you mean? You don't have the pictures?
**Scott:** Look!
**Vega:** Goodbye, my friends. See you again sometime, someplace. Thanks for the ride.

# Big Deal!

**Stephanie:** Yes?
**James:** Is Mr. Vidal at home?
**Stephanie:** Why?
**James:** We're ... uh ... business associates.
**Kevin:** Uh, I'm Kevin and this is James.
**Stephanie:** Daddy's by the pool.
**James:** The pool?
**Stephanie:** Yeah, it's that way. Go around the house. Take the path through the trees. The pool's right in front of you.
**James:** Thank you.
**Stephanie:** You're welcome.

**James:** Kevin!

**Tony:** Lauren! Don't forget, call Mr. Olsen this afternoon. And cancel my appointment with Senator Brandt ... Frankie, the suit! ... And get me a flight to Vegas.
**Lauren:** Las Vegas. On Wednesday?
**Tony:** Yeah. That's good.
**James:** Mr. Vidal?
**Tony:** Who are you?
**James:** We're from Mr. Olsen. You have some merchandise for him.
**Tony:** That's all, Frankie. Same time next week, huh? Lauren, take that dog for a walk. The computers are in the garage. I'd like the money first.
**James:** We have instructions from Mr. Olsen. First, the computers, then the money.
**Tony:** OK, guys. Right this way.

**Tony:** There you go, guys. One hundred and twenty computers. First-class merchandise. See you by the pool in one hour. Then I'd like the money, you understand? And be careful with those. Oh, and remember, that dog's dangerous.

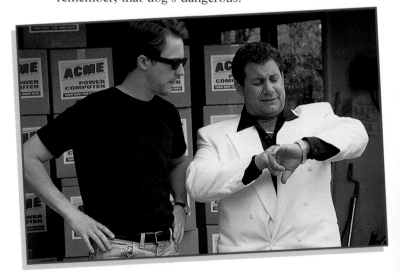

**Kevin:** Nice guy.
**James:** A hundred and twenty cartons. Come on, Kevin. That's sixty for me, and sixty for you.

**Tony:** They're here right now ... so, what about my money, Olsen? Yeah, sure, sure, I know that.

**Tony:** Lauren?
**Lauren:** Yes, Mr. Vidal?
**Tony:** I'd like lunch.
**Lauren:** Yes, Mr. Vidal. What would you like?
**Tony:** A salad.
**Lauren:** Chef's salad? Caesar? Niçoise? Waldorf? Russian?
**Tony:** I'd like ...uh ... the niçoise.

Lauren: Would you like olives with that today?

Tony: Forget the olives. I'm on a diet.

Lauren: Would you like French dressing on that?

Tony: No, give me some of that Thousand Island dressing.

Lauren: Mr. Vidal, what about your diet? Thousand Island has a lot of calories.

Tony: Lauren. I would like Thousand Island!

Lauren: You are the boss, Mr. Vidal.

Tony: And a T-Bone steak with French fries.

Tony: …then I'd like ice cream.

Lauren: Which flavor would you like?

Tony: What do we have?

Lauren: Chocolate. Strawberry. Vanilla.

Tony: OK, vanilla. And coffee.

James: That's it. Get the money, Kevin.

James: We have your money, Mr. Vidal. Would you like to count it now?

Tony: Guys! I'm having lunch! Go wait in the truck.

Stephanie: Would you like a drink?

Kevin: Could we have some water? We're real thirsty.

Tony: Hey! This isn't a restaurant!

Stephanie: Daddy, it's only water.

Tony: Water? They'd like water, huh? There's water in the pool!

James: Hey, Mr. Vidal! We have another appointment.

Tony: You wait for me. You understand?

Kevin: Yeah. Swim for it!

Tony: Lauren! The money!

Lauren: I can't swim.

Tony: Lauren …

Lauren: Mr. Vidal!

# Office Blues

First Man: Hi, Bruno

Second Man: Hi, Bruno.

Laura: Yes? Oh, no! It's Bruno.

Samuel: Don't say anything!

Laura: Answer the door.

Samuel: Hi, Bruno. How are you doing?

Bruno: Hi, Samuel. Can I come in?

Samuel: Oh, sure. Sure. Yeah, come right in.

Laura: Bruno! Oh, Olivia Revere is looking for you. She's in her office.

Bruno: But I'm real busy, Laura. I'm doing some work for Mr. Sikorski.

Laura: She's waiting for you, Bruno.

Bruno: OK. I'm going right now.

Laura: That's a great tie!

Bruno: Thank you. It's new.

Laura: This is nice … Oh! Ms. Revere!

Olivia: Bruno. Hello. Bruno, I have some work for you. Can you photocopy these reports for me, and those? Can you begin right now? I'd like them before five o'clock. Do you have a problem with that?

Bruno: Uh, no. I can do that. No problem.

Olivia: Good.

Samuel: Something wrong?

Bruno: I have all that work for Mr. Sikorski, and now all this work for Ms. Revere.

Samuel: So?

Bruno: I'm not going to finish it today.

Samuel: Mmm. Can you stay late tonight?

Bruno: Not really, it's my birthday today. I'm twenty-one.

Samuel: Hey, congratulations!

Bruno: Thanks. Uh, you see, my mom and dad are in New York, just for three days. I'm going to meet them tonight. They're going to be here at five o'clock. We're going to have dinner and see a show.

Samuel: It's only two thirty. You can do it.

Bruno: You think so?

Samuel: Sure. You can finish before five.

Laura: Bruno! What are you doing here?

Bruno: I have some reports. Ms. Revere wants copies this afternoon.

Laura: Ah. You can't.

Bruno: I don't understand.

Laura: Uh, you can't use the copier.

Bruno: Why? Are you using it? I can wait.

Laura: Uh. No, I'm not using it. It, uh … it isn't working.

Bruno: What's wrong with it?

Laura: I don't know. I'm waiting for the repair person.

Bruno: Maybe I can fix it.

Laura: No, no, you can't fix it. The repair person's going to be here soon.

Bruno: Instant Copy, East 34th Street … Print Quick, Lexington Avenue … Fast Copy …

Samuel: What are you doing?

Bruno: I'm looking for a photocopy shop. Is there one near here?

Samuel: But the repair person's fixing the copier right now.

**Bruno:** It's four o'clock! I can't wait. I'm going to call my mom and dad.

**Samuel:** No, don't do that!

**Bruno:** What am I going to do then? (*a phone rings*) Yes?

**Samuel:** Yes? Uh, this is Samuel speaking. ... Who is this? ... Oh, right ... Sure, I'm going to tell him right now ... Thanks. The copier's OK. It's working.

**Bruno:** Great!

**Everyone:** Happy birthday to you!
Happy birthday to you!
Happy birthday, dear Bruno,
Happy birthday to you!

**Everyone:** Happy birthday, Bruno!

**Olivia:** Bruno, what about my reports?

**Bruno:** Oh. Um ...

**Olivia:** Relax, Bruno. I'm kidding!

# The Websters

**Chelsea:** Tuesday, May twenty-third ... the beginning of another beautiful day ... Oh, hi. I'm Chelsea Webster. And I live in Westfield, New Jersey. This is my room.

**Mrs. Webster:** Chelsea! Chelsea!

**Chelsea:** That's my mom. My mom always gets up first.

**Mrs. Webster:** Chelsea! It's seven o'clock. Come on down!

**Chelsea:** Come and meet my family.

**Chelsea:** This is Mikey. He's my brother. Hi, Mikey.

**Mikey:** Hi, Chelsea.

**Chelsea:** Mikey always does his homework at breakfast.

**Mikey:** Hey, Chelsea. Can I borrow your calculator?

**Chelsea:** Don't you have one?

**Mikey:** It's at school. Can I borrow yours?

**Chelsea:** No way.

**Mikey:** But I can't do my math.

**Chelsea:** Tough. He always borrows my stuff. And he never gives it back.

**Mr. Webster:** Hi, Chelsea. Hi, Michael.

**Chelsea:** Hi, Dad

**Mikey:** Hi, Dad.

**Mr. Webster:** Is that your homework, Michael?

**Mikey:** I can't do it. I don't have a calculator.

**Mr. Webster:** You can borrow Chelsea's.

**Chelsea:** I don't believe this! Dad! My dad never listens to me.

**Chelsea:** Breakfast in America. For breakfast, I usually have some orange juice and some yogurt. Sometimes I have toast. And on weekends we usually cook a hot breakfast. Mmm ... strawberry. My favorite.

**Mrs. Webster:** Chelsea! Hi.

**Chelsea:** My mom works in the college library. She hardly ever eats breakfast.

**Mrs. Webster:** Do we have any strawberry yogurt?

**Chelsea:** Mmm, no, sorry. This is the last one.

**Mrs. Webster:** I hardly ever eat breakfast.

**Chelsea:** We don't usually speak at breakfast. Mikey? Mikey? My calculator! Mikey! Don't take my calculator, Mikey! OK, How often do you fight with your brother?

**Chelsea:** Hi, Mr. Carter.

**Mr. Carter:** Hello, Chelsea. Good morning, Chris, good morning, Jackie.

**Mr. Webster:** Hi, Bobby. How are you doing?

**Mrs. Webster:** Hey, Bobby.

**Chelsea:** Mr. Carter's our neighbor. He and my dad work downtown, so they carpool ... they share the ride. Sometimes my dad takes his car and sometimes Mr. Carter drives. This morning, it's Mr. Carter's turn. Uh, oh. This is Eric. He lives down the street. Eric has a car ... and sometimes he stops by and takes me to school.

**Chelsea:** Oh, hi, Eric.

**Eric:** Hi, Chelsea. How are you doing? Do you want a ride?

**Chelsea:** OK.

**Mr. Webster:** Eric! Are you going to the game tonight?

**Eric:** Sure, Mr. Webster.

**Mr. Carter:** How's it going, buddy?

**Eric:** Great, Mr. Carter.

**Mr. Webster:** 'Bye, Chelsea. Have a good day. See you at seven, Jackie!

**Mr. Carter:** See you later.

**Mrs. Webster:** Eric, come in and sit down.

**Chelsea:** Eric likes me – you know what I mean? My mom and dad like Eric ... and he likes them. I guess Eric's OK, but ... is that the time? Where's my stuff?

**Eric:** 'Bye, Mrs. Webster.

**Chelsea:** 'Bye, Mom.

**Mrs. Webster:** 'Bye, Chelsea. 'Bye, Eric.

**Chelsea:** Well, that's all, folks. Have a nice day.

# Good Morning, Greenstown

**Greg Tyler:** Good morning, Greenstown… This is the Good Morning Show with Greg Tyler. Nine to one weekdays. Having a good time here on…

**Jingle:** W H A T Greenstown… Greenstown… Greenstown.

**Greg:** Are you having a good time? We're all having a good time down here at W H A T Greenstown! This is Greg Tyler, your morning DJ at ten thirty-two. And the weather outside? It's a warm seventy-three on the street. And the forecast for today is sunny skies all day… can you believe that? And right now, if you're fighting the freeway, relax… here's Tanisha.

**Greg:** Marcie! Where are the questions for the quiz?
**Marcie:** Greg, they're right in front of you.
**Greg:** Hey! These are yesterday's!
**Marcie:** They were there a moment ago.
**Greg:** They aren't here now. What do I do?
**Marcie:** Look in the trash. That was my breakfast.

**Greg:** That was Tanisha's new single. It's a big hit. She was number nine last week. She's number five this week. Is she going to be number one next week? Listen to the Top Twenty Countdown on Saturday night at nine on…

**Jingle:** W H A T Greenstown… Greenstown… Greenstown.

**Greg:** You're listening to Greg Tyler. It's ten thirty-five, and it's time for … the Greg Tyler Rock Quiz, your chance to win this week's top ten CDs. Pick up the phone and call 5 3 5 W H A T now …

**Greg:** And our first caller's on the line. Your name, please?
**Tom:** Tom Altman.
**Greg:** Hi there, Tom. Where are you calling from?
**Tom:** The corner of 55th and Skyline Avenue. I'm a cab driver. I'm taking my coffee break.
**Greg:** OK. I have your first question here. What was Elvis Presley's first number one record?
**Tom:** Elvis. Uh, was that… uh…"Jailhouse Rock"?
**Greg:** Oh, no, it wasn't, Tom. Too bad!

**Greg:** Our next caller is…?
**Crystal:** Crystal Silvestri. And I know the answer… it was "Heartbreak Hotel."
**Greg:** And that's… the right answer, Crystal.
**Crystal:** Wow!
**Greg:** Next question, Crystal. Take it easy. Crystal, where are you calling from?
**Crystal:** Lakeside.

**Greg:** Lakeside? OK. Here's your question, Crystal. Who were the four members of… the Beatles.
**Crystal:** John, Paul, George and Ringo.
**Greg:** That's correct!
**Crystal:** Wow!
**Greg:** What kind of music do you listen to, Crystal?
**Crystal:** Heavy metal. Titanium's my favorite band.
**Greg:** Did you go to their concert Friday night?
**Crystal:** Yeah, I did. I was right up front. Did you go?
**Greg:** No, I didn't. It's not my kind of music, Crystal! So, the third and final question is… When did Buddy Holly die?
**Crystal:** He died in 1959… in a plane crash on February third at one fifty am, near Mason City, Iowa.
**Greg:** Wow, Crystal. The prize is yours!
**Crystal:** Wow!
**Greg:** That was Crystal Silvestri, our winner for today on the Greg Tyler Rock Quiz here on…

**Jingle:** W H A T Greenstown… Greenstown… Greenstown.

**Greg:** It's ten forty, and we have an interview with movie star Paloma Lee after the commercials. Stay with us.

**Greg:** Have a seat, Ms. Lee.
**Paloma:** Please, Paloma.
**Greg:** Paloma. Welcome to W H A T.

**Greg:** This is Greg Tyler, and with me right now I have movie star Paloma Lee. Paloma flew into Greenstown last night. She went to the Premiere of her new movie, "Swim Free" at the MCM Movie Theater. It's a fantastic movie, and I really enjoyed it. Tell us about the movie, Paloma.
**Paloma:** Thank you, Greg. We did the movie in Florida. It was a lot of fun. My costar was really cute.
**Greg:** Your costar?

**Paloma:** Yeah. Donny. We had a lot of scenes together. We became great friends.

**Greg:** Did he go to the Premiere with you last night?

**Paloma:** Excuse me?

**Greg:** Did Donny come with you to Greenstown?

**Paloma:** No... You didn't see the movie last night, did you?

**Greg:** Donny is a... dolphin?

**Paloma:** That's right, Greg. Donny is a dolphin.

**Greg:** And are you going to make another movie with Donny?

**Paloma:** Donny is a wild animal, Greg. We released him in the ocean after the movie. He's "swimming free."

**Greg:** Uh, huh. That's a beautiful story, Paloma. And the next record's for you, Donny ... wherever you are.

# The Artist

**Gallery Owner:** Good morning. Can I help you?

**The Artist:** Yes, thank you. Are you the owner?

**Gallery Owner:** Yes.

**The Artist:** I want to show you my work.

**Gallery Owner:** And you want to exhibit it here?

**The Artist:** Yes!

**Gallery Owner:** Let me see it, then.

**The Artist:** I was at art school in Kansas City. I came to New York last week. I'm trying to sell my pictures.

**Gallery Owner:** Hmm. This is interesting. But I'm sorry. We can't exhibit it here. You see, we only exhibit well-known artists. May I suggest something?

**The Artist:** Yes.

**Gallery Owner:** Why don't you spend some time in the art museums here in New York? Study some of the great paintings ... then who knows? Maybe I'll see you in a year or two, mm?

**The Artist:** Thank you for your time.

**Gallery Owner:** You're welcome.

**Woman:** That's a Stroheim, isn't it?

**Man:** Yes. Brilliant. It's a work of genius. A friend of mine bought a Stroheim. It cost two hundred thousand dollars, and it was only a pencil cartoon.

**Woman:** Oh, really? How much is this one worth?

**Man:** The museum paid ten million, I believe. That was twenty years ago. Of course, Stroheim lived in Paris for many years, and he painted in different styles. He painted this one in 1947.

**Woman:** Fascinating.

**Man:** Let's go and look at the Andy Warhols.

**Guard:** So, what do you think of it?

**The Artist:** It's very ... interesting. Do you like it?

**Guard:** No way. My kid sister paints pictures like that, and she's only three years old.

**Gallery Owner:** This is new, isn't it?

**Art Critic:** Mmm. It's another Stroheim. He painted in so many different styles. I love this one!

**Gallery Owner:** Yes, it's good ... it's very good.

**Art Critic:** Brilliant!

**Gallery Owner:** Funny. It looks familiar. Ah, well, I want to see the Picassos. I'll see you later.

**Art Critic:** I'll meet you by the entrance.

**Guard:** My kid sister paints pictures like that, and she's only three years old.

**Art Critic:** I'm an art critic. I write for the "New York Times."

**The Artist:** Oh.

**Art Critic:** This is a very fine painting.

**The Artist:** Mm, yes, I agree with you.

**Art Critic:** Nice meeting you.

**The Artist:** Yes!

Rock Quiz answers – page 64
Thursday's questions
1C 2A 3C 4 B
Wednesday's questions
1 B 2 C 3 A 4 B